LeBron James

LeBron James

by Anne Wallace Sharp

LUCENT BOOKS

An imprint of Thomson Gale, a part of The Thomson Corporation

THOMSON
™
GALE

Detroit • New York • San Francisco • New Haven, Conn. • Waterville, Maine • London

THOMSON

★ ™

GALE

© 2008 Thomson Gale, a part of The Thomson Corporation.

Thomson and Star Logo are trademarks and Gale and Lucent Books are registered trademarks used herein under license.

For more information, contact:
Lucent Books
27500 Drake Rd.
Farmington Hills, MI 48331-3535
Or you can visit our Internet site at http://www.gale.com

LIBRARY OF CONGRESS CATALOGING-IN-PUBLICATION DATA

Sharp, Anne Wallace.
  LeBron James / by Anne Wallace Sharp.
    p. cm. — (People in the news)
  Includes bibliographical references and index.
  ISBN-13: 978-1-4205-0014-1 (hardcover)
  1. James, LeBron—Juvenile literature. 2. Basketball players—United States—
Biography—Juvenile literature. I. Title.
  GV884.J36S49 2008
  796.323092—dc22
  [B]
                                                                        2007024775

ISBN-10: 1-4205-0014-7

Printed in the United States of America

Contents

Fame and celebrity are alluring. People are drawn to those who walk in fame's spotlight, whether they are known for great accomplishments or for notorious deeds. The lives of the famous pique public interest and attract attention, perhaps because their experiences seem in some ways so different from, yet in other ways so similar to, our own.

Newspapers, magazines, and television regularly capitalize on this fascination with celebrity by running profiles of famous people. For example, television programs such as *Entertainment Tonight* devote all their programming to stories about entertainment and entertainers. Magazines such as *People* fill their pages with stories of the private lives of famous people. Even newspapers, newsmagazines, and television news frequently delve into the lives of well-known personalities. Despite the number of articles and programs, few provide more than a superficial glimpse at their subjects.

Lucent's People in the News series offers young readers a deeper look into the lives of today's newsmakers, the influences that have shaped them, and the impact they have had in their fields of endeavor and on other people's lives. The subjects of the series hail from many disciplines and walks of life. They include authors, musicians, athletes, political leaders, entertainers, entrepreneurs, and others who have made a mark on modern life and who, in many cases, will continue to do so for years to come.

These biographies are more than factual chronicles. Each book emphasizes the contributions, accomplishments, or deeds that have brought fame or notoriety to the individual and shows how that person has influenced modern life. Authors portray their subjects in a realistic, unsentimental light. For example, Bill Gates —the cofounder and chief executive officer of the software giant Microsoft—has been instrumental in making personal computers the most vital tool of the modern age. Few dispute his business savvy, his perseverance, or his technical expertise, yet critics say he is ruthless in his dealings with competitors and driven more by his desire to maintain Microsoft's dominance in the computer industry than by an interest in furthering technology.

In these books, young readers will encounter inspiring stories about real people who achieved success despite enormous obstacles. Oprah Winfrey—the most powerful, most watched, and wealthiest woman on television today—spent the first six years of her life in the care of her grandparents while her unwed mother sought work and a better life elsewhere. Her adolescence was colored by promiscuity, pregnancy at age fourteen, rape, and sexual abuse.

Each author documents and supports his or her work with an array of primary and secondary source quotations taken from diaries, letters, speeches, and interviews. All quotes are footnoted to show readers exactly how and where biographers derive their information and provide guidance for further research. The quotations enliven the text by giving readers eyewitness views of the life and accomplishments of each person covered in the People in the News series.

In addition, each book in the series includes photographs, annotated bibliographies, timelines, and comprehensive indexes. For both the casual reader and the student researcher, the People in the News series offers insight into the lives of today's newsmakers—people who shape the way we live, work, and play in the modern age.

A Prodigy

A prodigy is someone, especially a child or young adult, who has special or unusual skill or talent in a specific area. For instance, children who master a musical instrument at an early age are said to be child prodigies. In basketball, LeBron James is a prodigy.

In order to become that prodigy, LeBron overcame numerous hardships. He was born and raised in the slums of Akron, Ohio, and was the only child of a single mother. During his early life he was surrounded by poverty and at times even lived on handouts from friends. Despite these factors, he emerged from the deprivations of childhood to become an extraordinary athlete. After outstanding performances in summer basketball camps, LeBron earned national recognition for his athletic skills during his high school career. While attending St. Vincent–St. Mary High School in Akron, LeBron led a talented team to three state championships.

In doing so, he caught the eye of the national media and was compared to basketball superstar Michael Jordan, who many sports analysts have called the greatest player who ever played the game. Sports writer Michelle Kaufman, in December 2002 during LeBron's senior year in high school, elaborates:

> LeBron has been on the cover of *Sports Illustrated,* under the headline: The Chosen One. Letterman wants him. He has Michael Jordan's cell phone number and has played in His Airness' top secret workouts. James's games are televised on ESPN 2 and pay-per-view. His autograph is for sale on eBay

As a basketball prodigy, LeBron James displayed the skills of a seasoned professional while still in high school.

($42) as are tickets for upcoming games ($100 each). Nike and Adidas are dangling $20 million contracts in his baby face and NBA scouts predict he will be the top pick in the 2003 draft. He is 17 years old. He has yet to pick a prom date. Already he has agents, shoe company executives, NBA scouts, reporters, and fans chasing him.[1]

LeBron was being promoted as the best high school basketball player ever, and a sure bet to become professional basketball's next superstar.

In addition to the attention earned on the basketball court, LeBron also came under scrutiny for two incidents that occurred during his senior year. His mother presented him with a new Hummer vehicle for his eighteenth birthday. This made the Ohio High School Athletic Association suspicious that the car was a gift from a sports company. Shortly after this matter was settled to the James's satisfaction, another incident marred LeBron's reputation. He accepted two jerseys from a sporting goods store, in violation of amateur athletic rules that does not allow such gifts. After a brief suspension that threatened to end his high school career, the Ohio High School Athletic Association ruled in LeBron's favor. Other than these two incidents, LeBron's high school years passed without problems.

Since his high school graduation, LeBron has won almost every award given in the National Basketball Association. During his four seasons playing for the Cleveland Cavaliers, LeBron has won accolade after accolade. He has won Rookie of the Year honors, has been selected to play in three All-Star games, has led his team to two playoff seasons, and has been chosen to represent the United States on the 2008 Olympics basketball team.

Despite his superstar status, LeBron has remained humble, never forgetting his roots. He has committed himself to giving back to his community in the form of charitable ventures that benefit the youth of Cleveland and Akron. He has also become a dedicated and loving father, pledging to give his son a good family foundation.

Biographer Ryan Jones summarizes LeBron's extraordinary life:

> For every critical word written or uttered about him or his family or the people around him, and for every malignant assumption made about the reasons for and rewards of his success, LeBron has only been guilty of two things: saying yes on a few occasions when he might have been better off saying no, and playing basketball with as great a combination of instinct and athleticism and competitiveness and joy as anyone ever has.[2]

James, himself, sums up his success in one sentence: "Basketball is my life, and if I told you something different, I'd be telling you a lie."[3]

Chapter 1

Overcoming Poverty and Deprivation

LeBron Raymone James was born on December 30, 1984, in Akron, Ohio, to Gloria James. His childhood was characterized by poverty and deprivation as Gloria, a single mother, struggled to make ends meet. Never sure of where he was laying his head each night, LeBron nonetheless grew into a conscientious youth who was determined to succeed. He had much to overcome in his first dozen years. His salvation came in the form of sports, which provided much of the only stability that LeBron experienced in his youth.

In his youth, LeBron often played basketball on run-down courts such as this one.

"My Mother's My Everything"

Gloria James, LeBron's mother, was a sixteen-year-old high school student who lived at home with her mother Freda and her two brothers, Terry and Curt, when she discovered she was pregnant.

Gloria James, pictured right, provided the love and stability LeBron needed while he was growing up.

Gloria, despite her youth and circumstances, pledged that she would provide the best home possible for her infant son, LeBron. With her mother and brothers helping to provide care for her son, Gloria quit school and tried to find steady employment to help pay the bills.

However, as an unskilled worker, Gloria found little success in the job market, drifting from job to job and often ending up in the unemployment lines. Despite her difficult situation, she proved to be a loving mother, doing everything in her power to raise LeBron and provide as much stability as possible for her young son. "Despite her failings," states one Internet source, "Gloria worked hard to be a loving mother and shield LeBron from the poverty and violence of the streets. This was no easy chore . . . "[4]

LeBron has long credited his mother with being the most stabilizing influence in his life. Their love for each other helped them endure tragedies, challenges, and pitfalls along the way. Even today, with LeBron firmly enthroned as a superstar in the National Basketball Association (NBA), Gloria still refers to him as "my baby" or "Bron-Bron." LeBron calls his mom the most significant person in his life and has her name tattooed on his biceps. "My mother is my everything," LeBron states. "Always has been. Always will be."[5]

While his mother was ever present, LeBron's biological father was never a part of the youngster's life. According to family sources, LeBron's father was a skilled street ball player and ex-convict who wanted no part in being a father or a family man. To this day, both LeBron and his mother refuse to speak about his father.

Hickory Street

LeBron and his mother spent his first few years of life living in the home of his grandmother Freda James. Their house was located on Hickory Street in the middle of a tough neighborhood in Akron, Ohio. The area was filled with trash piles where old tires, bathtubs, and other items were illegally dumped. Many city officials referred to the street and neighborhood as an eyesore and had future plans to demolish many of the homes located there.

Despite these circumstances, LeBron's grandmother, a single mother herself, was a strong woman who offered both Gloria and LeBron a good home. Sports biographer David Lee Morgan claims that Freda helped her daughter nurture LeBron "with a fierceness of someone who had already struggled through poverty and disrespect her entire life."[6]

Finances were extremely tight for the entire James family. Most of the residents in the neighborhood earned minimum wage and the James family was no exception. There was seldom enough money to pay the mortgage and other bills. With the unemployment rate particularly high in that section of Akron, the neighbors learned to work together and help each other. Community members, though living in poverty themselves, helped Gloria and her son by donating what food and clothing they could spare.

Eddie Jackson

LeBron's grandmother, Freda, was like many others in the neighborhood and often opened her home to anyone who needed a temporary place to stay. One of those who benefited from her kindness was a young man named Eddie Jackson. Eddie moved into the Jameses' house when LeBron was eight months old. A few years older than Gloria, Eddie had excelled in sports in school and was, at the time, unemployed.

Eddie and Gloria soon started dating and he quickly became very attached to Gloria's son. LeBron grew to love Eddie, and to this day considers him to be the only father he has. Years later, when LeBron began winning awards for his athletic skills, he always thanked his mother Gloria and his father Eddie for all the love and support they had provided.

While living with the James family, Eddie often spent his spare time playing with LeBron. He and the toddler spent hours playing games and wrestling on the floor. Eddie speaks of those experiences with affection: "You could be laying on the floor and

Eddie Jackson

Eddie Jackson, a young man who often lived with LeBron James and his family, played a significant role in the life of young LeBron. Eddie fulfilled the role of father and provided love and support for LeBron, whose own father was never a part of his childhood. Eddie tried to always be present for LeBron, although he was not always successful.

Eddie Jackson was a loving father figure when LeBron was growing up.

Eddie, like LeBron's mother Gloria, struggled to make ends meet and often got into trouble. While most people who knew Eddie considered him to be basically a good guy, Eddie had a habit of making bad decisions. In 1990, for instance, when LeBron was six years old, Eddie was sent to prison for trafficking cocaine near a neighborhood school. He went to prison again in 2002 after pleading guilty to mortgage and mail fraud. In David Lee Morgan's book *LeBron James: The Rise of a Star*, the author elaborates on Eddie's character: "Eddie was a charming hustler, a man who had served time in prison for selling drugs ... but he loved Gloria, adored her son, and vowed to always be there for LeBron. He didn't always succeed, but LeBron loved him for his effort."[1]

Eddie, for all his faults, wanted to make sure LeBron didn't make the same mistakes that he had. Years later, and quoted in Morgan's book, Eddie stated, "I made sure he didn't do the things I did. We [Gloria and I] protected him and made sure he was around the right people to prevent him from making the mistakes that some of us did."[2]

1 David Lee Morgan. *LeBron James: The Rise of a Star.* Cleveland: Gray and Company, 2003, p. 15.
2 Quoted in Morgan. *LeBron James: The Rise of a Star,* p. 131.

the next thing you know LeBron is jumping up and down on the couch and he'd jump right on you."[7] It was Eddie who convinced Gloria to buy toddler LeBron a toy basketball set for Christmas. Both of them happened to have jobs at the time so they were able to combine their money to buy the youngster a complete basketball set that included a backboard, ball, hoop, and stand that could be used indoors.

As the two of them were setting up the toy together on Christmas Eve, Eddie and Gloria heard a loud thump in the house and hurried to see what had happened. They found Freda James on the floor. She died shortly thereafter in Eddie's arms from a heart attack. Eddie and Gloria decided not to tell LeBron about his grandmother's death until after the holidays so that the child could enjoy Christmas morning and his new toy. LeBron was overjoyed with his present and played with it most of the day. He especially liked to dunk the ball while jumping as high as he could.

Elizabeth Park

After Freda's death, the situation for Gloria, Eddie, and LeBron deteriorated rapidly. Gloria was still only nineteen years old, while her brother Terry was twenty-two and Curt only twelve. Money was virtually nonexistent. Their neighbors on Hickory Street offered what they could but there was no way Gloria could pay the mortgage on their decrepit home. As a result, the bank soon foreclosed on their mortgage (took back the property because it was bought with borrowed money that was not being paid back) and turned the house over to the city of Akron. The house was eventually condemned by the city and destroyed.

The James family and Eddie were forced to move. Terry and Curt left to live together and fend for themselves, as did Eddie, while Gloria and LeBron went to live temporarily with an aunt. Biographer Jones describes the effect that Freda's death had on Gloria and LeBron: "That loss led Gloria and LeBron into a tenuous existence of little familial support, great financial uncertainty, and increasing instability that saw the mother and

Akron, Ohio, was LeBron's birthplace.

son family unit constantly on the move, usually through the city's roughest neighborhoods."[8]

Unable to stay permanently with the aunt, Gloria was forced to find another place for herself and her small son to live. She and LeBron eventually moved to a housing project called Elizabeth Park, a complex that was old and long past its prime. The area consisted of hundreds of brick row houses with large areas of open space where the children could play. Morgan describes the area: "Elizabeth Park was a place to warehouse low-income black residents of all ages and backgrounds."[9]

It was also an area where drugs, alcohol, and crime were big problems. The Akron police made frequent visits to Elizabeth Park to help combat drive-by shootings and gang fights. It was a tough neighborhood for a young boy to grow up in. Every day,

LeBron saw drug deals going down. He also witnessed occasional shootings and even a couple of murders. As a teenager, LeBron spoke about his childhood: "I've seen a lot of stuff that kids my age just don't see."[10]

Their years at Elizabeth Park were characterized by instability and desperation. One biographer summarizes:

> Life was often a struggle for LeBron and his mother. Gloria battled personal problems during much of his childhood . . . Bouncing between retail and accounting jobs, Gloria was never able to land steady work, and she and LeBron moved from apartment to apartment.[11]

Despite this, Gloria and LeBron managed to survive. They lived at Elizabeth Park off and on for more than six years, moving from one friend's home to another, never actually having a place to call their own. In one year alone, when LeBron was five years old, they moved a total of seven times. As had happened on Hickory Street, LeBron and his mother credit the help of community members for enabling them to survive.

The Walkers

As a result of the unstable situation in which he lived, at times LeBron struggled to cope, especially in school. There was little incentive for LeBron to go to school and, as a result, during his fourth-grade year, he skipped many days of classes, preferring instead to stay home and play. After Christmas break that year, he decided not to go back to school at all. Gloria did not know quite what to do, and she reached out to friends for a solution. She spoke honestly about the situation and also admitted that she needed time away from her child and her responsibilities to try to get her life back together.

Jones elaborates on what could have happened: "At that point, with a struggling single mother, no steady income, no place he could really call home and little motivation at school, it would've been awfully easy for LeBron to fall through the proverbial crack."[12] Instead, Gloria turned to Frankie Walker Sr., a man she knew through some of LeBron's after-school activities. She asked if the Walkers would allow LeBron to live with them for a while.

Despite already having three children of their own, the Walkers opened their home to LeBron, who moved in with the family for the rest of his fourth-grade school year. For the next two years, LeBron lived with the Walkers during the week and then spent time with his mother on the weekends. LeBron has often spoken of that time in his life, "It was like a new beginning for me. When I moved in with the Walkers, I went from missing eighty-seven days my fourth-grade year to zero days in the fifth grade . . . I love them. They are like my family . . . I wouldn't be here without them."[13]

LeBron thrived in his new home environment. Up to that point, there had been nothing but chaos and confusion in his life because of the constant moving he and his mother had done. Now at the Walkers, there was consistency in his life. LeBron also learned about discipline and responsibility. Just like the Walker children, LeBron had certain chores he was expected to do around the house. The Walkers also gave the youngster plenty of attention and affection. They always celebrated LeBron's birthday and had regular holiday celebrations that included LeBron and his mother. Even today, when money is no longer an issue, LeBron and his mother spend Thanksgiving with the Walkers.

"I'm an A Student in Basketball"

While LeBron also played football as a child and teenager, he loved basketball the most. It was Frankie Walker Sr. who first put a basketball in LeBron's hands and encouraged the youngster to practice on the backboard and net installed in the Walker's driveway. Walker coached organized basketball in a recreation league at the Summit Lake Community Center in Akron, an inner city center where boys and girls could learn to play various sports. Walker was a solid mentor for LeBron.

Walker began teaching LeBron how to play basketball and passed on his considerable knowledge of the game to the eager youngster. The coach discovered that LeBron, then a fourth-grader, was a natural and gifted young athlete. "I had never coached a kid who picked things up and excelled in them as quickly as LeBron . . .," Walker stated. "He began to approach the game of basketball the way a chess master approaches chess."[14] LeBron's ability to learn the game was a quality and trait that would follow him throughout his playing career.

LeBron was thrilled when he was invited to join Walker's recreation league. He spent hours on the practice court, shooting the basketball from every imaginable position. Even as a fourth-grader, LeBron was already showing leadership skills that he would continue to develop in the years ahead. When LeBron

Peewee Football

LeBron's first real introduction and exposure to sports came through playing Peewee football when he was in the fourth grade. He played for a team called the South Rangers. The team was coached by Bruce Kelker, a man who wanted to pass on his football knowledge to area youngsters. LeBron had no experience other than street ball, but he still picked up on the game quickly. In his first season with the South Rangers, for instance, LeBron scored eighteen touchdowns for the team, mainly playing tailback and catching passes. Kelker was amazed at the youngster's hands—how easily he was able to catch even hard-to-reach passes. As quoted in David Lee Morgan's book *LeBron James: The Rise of a Star*, Kelker states, ". . . I had never coached a kid who picked up the knowledge of the game so quick."[1]

LeBron talks fondly of his days of Peewee football. He is quoted in Morgan's book as saying, "The South Rangers meant a lot to me. All the coaches and parents really cared about us, and they made playing the game fun."[2] LeBron played football each year thereafter until the end of the eleventh grade.

1 Quoted in David Lee Morgan. *LeBron James: The Rise of a Star*. Cleveland: Gray and Company, 2003, p. 31.
2 Quoted in Morgan. *LeBron James: The Rise of a Star*, p. 32.

entered the fifth grade, Walker was so impressed with LeBron's skills and knowledge of the game that he made the youngster an assistant coach of the fourth-grade team. He told the other parents that LeBron, even at his young age, could already offer basketball insights to younger players because of his natural abilities. LeBron commented on this move: "I'm an 'A' student in basketball. We are all blessed with the gifts that God gave us and it's important to use your gifts the right way."[15]

The Northeast Shooting Stars

In his fifth-grade year, after playing in Walker's recreation league, LeBron joined the Northeast Shooting Stars, a team that played in the Amateur Athletic Union (AAU). The AAU is one of the largest nonprofit sports organizations in the United States. "A multi-sport, event-driven organization," the Union's website states, "the AAU is dedicated exclusively to the promotion and development of amateur sports programs."[16] As part of its basketball program, the AAU offers numerous summer camps and tournaments for boys and girls. The various teams that participate in these programs compete locally for the most part, but they also enter state-wide and national tournaments.

The Shooting Star team was coached by a man who would become another of LeBron's most important mentors, Dru Joyce II. Joyce was dedicated to the game of basketball and devoted his time to coaching youngsters throughout the Akron area. As a result of his contact with Joyce, LeBron improved his basketball skills and also made new friendships.

The coach's son Dru Joyce III (known as Little Dru) introduced LeBron to Sian Cotton and later Willie McGee. Together, the four boys would later be christened the "Fabulous Four" by area basketball fans. They also formed a friendship that lasted throughout their high school years and beyond. LeBron relied on this inner circle for support, comradeship, and love. LeBron often speaks of this inner circle of friends "I've got this inner circle. I've had it for years. And if you haven't been in the circle since Day One, you're never going to be in it."[17] From that moment on, the four

Early Accolades

Coach Dru Joyce II, a father figure and mentor to young LeBron, was very impressed with LeBron and the youngster's innate athletic abilities on the basketball court from the beginning. In an article in the *Akron Beacon Journal* written by Terry Pluto, Joyce recalls: "By the time LeBron was in the ninth grade, I had pretty much taught him all I could."[1] Ryan Jones, author of *King James: Believe the Hype: The LeBron James Story*, describes how Joyce still talks about the "ten-year-old who never missed practice, who always wanted to learn, who wouldn't rest until he'd learned that jump shot that had frustrated him."[2]

Pluto also described how Joyce was also complimentary about LeBron's work ethic on the basketball court. "We were driving down East Avenue," Joyce stated. "I started telling LeBron about passing the ball, how great players make their teammates better . . . He was only eleven. That was the last time I ever had to talk about LeBron shooting too much. He just got it. He started passing the ball."[3]

The men who later coached LeBron, both at the high school and professional levels, praised James's early coaches, including Joyce. They told reporters how fortunate James had been to have men like Frankie Walker Sr., Dru Joyce, and Lee Cotton who taught him to play unselfishly and as part of a team.

1 Quoted in Terry Pluto. "LeBron James, Once a Lanky Kid, Has Come a Long Way to the NBA. *Akron Beacon Journal*, April 20, 2004.
2 Quoted in Ryan Jones. *King James: Believe the Hype: The LeBron James Story*. New York: St. Martin's Press, 2003, p. 36.
3 Quoted in Pluto. "LeBron James, Once a Lanky Kid ..."

boys would do everything together and refused to allow anything to get in the way of their friendship.

It was not long before the Shooting Stars made an impression on the national scene. They qualified for the Under Sixth Grade AAU National Championships in Salt Lake City, Utah. It was the first time any of the boys had played outside the state of Ohio.

The team made a good showing in their first tournament, placing tenth in a field of seventy-one. In August 1997, the boys, playing in Orlando, Florida, won the twelve-and-under division after competing against thirty-one other teams. LeBron was named the tournament's most valuable player. The four boys played great basketball together and, during their years of AAU play, won six national championships and more than two hundred games. Joyce explained the team's success: "They believed in themselves and each other." [18]

Chapter 2

The Chosen One

With a solid foundation in athletics and with his home life relatively stable, LeBron was ready to enter high school. He devoted most of the summer after his eighth-grade year to being with his friends. They went to the movies together, played games on his Sony Play Station 2, and spent hours on the basketball courts around Akron. LeBron also practiced alone daily, shooting hundreds of jump shots and working on his dribbling and free throws. Every Sunday, the foursome went to the Jewish Community Center in downtown Akron to attend a basketball clinic held there. The basketball program at the Center was run by former college coach Keith Dambrot. Little Dru talks about the reason the four friends chose to attend: "I just thought Coach Dambrot was a good coach and that I could learn a lot of stuff from him—that all four of us could."[19]

From the beginning, Dambrot and the other coaches at the Center were impressed with LeBron's basketball skills. One of the assistant coaches, Steve Culp, talked animatedly about James:

> . . . this kid is coming at me and wants to show me up . . . in the eighth grade. LeBron had that competitive spirit that you don't even see in college kids . . . I've seen a lot of great young players, but I had never seen a young kid like that before . . . He just got more competitive as it went on . . . This kid is going to be unreal.[20]

St. Vincent–St. Mary High School

Playing under Dambrot at the Jewish Community Center also influenced LeBron and his friends when it came time to decide

Keith Dambrot

Keith Dambrot, as the coach of the Jewish Community Center clinics in Akron and later St. Vincent–St. Mary High School, pinpointed LeBron's superb talent even before LeBron had entered high school. He also coached LeBron and his friends during their freshman year. That Dambrot was at St. Vincent–St. Mary at all was something of a miracle comeback.

Dambrot began coaching at Ashland (Ohio) University in 1989. His success there led to coaching positions at Tiffon (Ohio) University, Akron University, and Eastern Michigan University. In 1991, he was offered the head coaching position at Central Michigan University. Dambrot's career at this college was cut short when he became involved in a racial controversy. After using a racial insult to stir up the team (most of whom were black), Dambrot was suspended and then fired. Dambrot apologized repeatedly, saying that he had made a stupid and unprofessional mistake. In *King James: Believe the Hype: The LeBron James Story*, Ryan Jones quotes Dambrot as saying, "I didn't mean to hurt anybody, and it was not meant to be derogatory."[1] Unable to find another coaching position, he returned to his hometown of Akron where he kept a low profile as a stockbroker.

Dambrot's return to basketball came through the Jewish Community Center in Akron. As word spread of his professionalism, Dambrot's clinics grew in size, ultimately attracting LeBron and his friends. Finally, administrators at St. Vincent–St. Mary High School were willing to offer him a job.

1 Quoted in Ryan Jones. *King James: Believe the Hype: The LeBron James Story*. New York: St. Martin's Press, 2003, p. 30.

which high school they would attend in the fall. In Akron, the school board allows parents and incoming freshmen to choose the high school they want to attend. When the boys learned that Dambrot had been hired to coach the St. Vincent–St. Mary High School team, they decided to follow him to the school. As they entered their freshman year at St. Vincent, the four boys set a goal for themselves—winning a state championship for the school.

The school was a good choice for LeBron. St. Vincent–St. Mary High School, a small inner-city Catholic school, was best known for its academics; more than 90 percent of its seniors went to college. Due to its serious academic standards, LeBron was forced to keep up his grades so he could play sports. LeBron responded in an admirable fashion and made the honor roll on a number of occasions.

His teachers, coaches, advisors, and other students became an extended family for LeBron. One of his best high school friends was Maverick Carter, two years LeBron's senior. Carter was a star basketball player and a good friend to LeBron—the two were so close that, despite not being related, they called each other "cousin." Surrounded by his friends, involved in both football and basketball, and challenged to improve his grades, LeBron thrived and matured at the high school.

Football

While basketball was LeBron's best sport, he also excelled at football and played on the St. Vincent football team during his first three years of high school. He has since spoken of how much he loved the game: "For me it was just about getting out there and doing what I loved to do, which was play football."[21] By the time he was a junior, his football coach Jay Brophy told LeBron that he could probably make a career for himself in the National Football League (NFL).

In his freshman year, for instance, LeBron made an immediate impact on the team, and at age fourteen got significant playing time as a wide receiver. By the end of his first season of football, James had become one of the keys to St. Vincent's success on the field. The opposing coach in one of their games spoke of this: "LeBron ended up being their go-to guy, and holy smokes, he did a good job of stepping in."[22]

LeBron's skills improved during his next two years on the team. During his sophomore year, he caught more than forty passes for

LeBron played high school basketball for the St. Vincent–St. Mary Irish.

a total of 840 yards and eleven touchdowns. That year he was named to the Division IV all-Ohio team and was also chosen as St. Vincent's most valuable player. In his junior year, LeBron helped lead the team to the Ohio state semi-finals. He caught sixty-two passes that year while compiling more than twelve hundred yards. His coach Jim Meyer commented on his prowess: "He had the best hand-to-eye coordination and the best reflexes I'd ever seen. He did things that can't be taught. He just grabbed footballs out of the sky."[23]

Gloria James attended all of LeBron's football games, fully supporting his decision to play the sport. However, she also had a deep-seated fear that he would be injured and, in the process, ruin his basketball career. Toward the end of LeBron's junior football season, Gloria's fears were realized when LeBron broke the index finger on his left hand in a post-season game. Fortunately, the injury was not severe enough to keep him off the basketball court. Because of this injury and his determination to play professional basketball, LeBron opted not to play football during his senior year.

Freshman Year Basketball

Despite his skill in football, it was on the basketball court that LeBron truly excelled and made a name for himself. Even as a freshman, LeBron was recognized as an up-and-coming player, as well as someone who was likely to make a career in professional basketball. After just a few high school games, Dambrot praised LeBron's already considerable skills: "LeBron reminded me of an athletic Magic Johnson. He could rebound, pass, and defend . . . My feeling was that if he wanted to be the best ever, he had the talent to be, as long as he worked hard."[24]

During LeBron's freshman year, the St. Vincent Irish team was led by senior Maverick Carter, LeBron's close friend and "cousin." While Carter was the star player for the Irish, LeBron added a great deal of talent to the team. With James playing point guard, the team went undefeated and headed to the state championship. Thanks in part to LeBron's twenty-five points, St. Vincent beat Jamestown Greenview High School for the Ohio state title.

After the game, Dambrot praised LeBron for his performance as a freshman. "LeBron is a basketball genius, there is no other way to see it."[25] Dambrot predicted that LeBron would continue to improve his skills and lead the team to other championships.

"He Keeps Getting Better"

During the summer between his freshman and sophomore years, LeBron grew another 3 inches (8cm), making him 6 feet 7 inches (2m 1cm) tall. After playing football in the fall, LeBron concentrated all his energy on basketball. A new boy had joined the team and, despite LeBron's insistence that it could not be done, quickly earned a spot in the "Fab Four's" inner circle. His name was Romeo Travis, a young man who complemented the rest of the team in every way. The Fabulous Four became the Fabulous Five and looked forward to another winning season. With LeBron leading the way, St. Vincent finished with a 27–1 record.

The team's only loss that year came at the hands of Oak Hill Academy, Virginia, by the close score of 79–78. LeBron was severely hampered in the game because of crippling back spasms. The pain caused his shooting to be slightly off the mark. Despite this, the game stayed close until the final seconds, with Oak Hill maintaining a small lead. As the game neared its end, the outcome rested on LeBron's shoulders, but he missed two free throws and a jump shot. St. Vincent lost. LeBron was devastated by the loss and said afterwards that he felt that he had let the entire team down. "I'm proud of everybody, the players, the coaches, the fans, everybody. We had a chance to win, but the shot just wouldn't go in."[26]

The St. Vincent Irish went undefeated for the remainder of the season and won the Ohio Division III State Championship. LeBron earned the tournament's Most Valuable Player award and, in addition, was named first team All-State. He also became the first sophomore in Ohio's history to win the state's Mr. Basketball award, an honor given to the most outstanding high school player in the state. *USA Today* named him to its first-team All-America high school team. By the end of the season, LeBron was ranked as one of the best high school basketball players in the country.

At the end of LeBron's sophomore year, Dambrot announced that he was leaving St. Vincent to return to college basketball. He had secured a job as head coach at the University of Akron. While the team was disappointed, they all acknowledged the great job Dambrot had done at St. Vincent. Dambrot himself spoke of his players: "Few coaches were ever blessed with such a collection of proven talent, let alone with a single all-world player.[27]

In telling reporters about his departure, Dambrot highly praised his star player, LeBron James:

Most guys that dominate at his age do it athletically, but LeBron has done it with skills and knowledge . . . He just understands the game . . . In order to get better at this game, you gotta be able to learn. The guy is amazing from that perspective and athletically, he keeps getting better, because he's just growing and maturing.[28]

"It Was Cool"

With LeBron's basketball skills continuing to improve each year, he and his family began to plan for the future. Family friend and sports enthusiast Chris Dennis approached LeBron, Gloria, and Eddie with suggestions that would improve LeBron's chances for a professional career. He told them that, in order for LeBron to get the proper acknowledgment he deserved, LeBron needed to play with the country's best players. His primary suggestion was getting LeBron involved in the American Athletic Union high school summer circuit, where LeBron would be exposed to college and professional scouts and coaches.

The AAU basketball camps have become increasingly important in the last two decades as a showcase for high school talent. Sports historian Jones elaborates: "Increasingly . . . as stringent NCAA regulations have limited the opportunity college coaches have to evaluate possible recruits during the high school season, the AAU circuit has taken on added significance."[29]

After listening to Dennis describe the benefits of the summer program, Gloria and Eddie readily agreed that LeBron should

Five-Star Camp

Summer basketball camps are an important part of a young player's training, as author David Lee Morgan describes in *LeBron James: The Rise of a Star:* "The biggest ones are gathering grounds for talented kids around the country to compete with each other, to pick up some of the finer points of the game and . . . to show off their stuff."[1] The camps are frequented by college and professional scouts alike.

One of the better-known summer camps that LeBron attended, Five-Star Camp, was in Pittsburgh, Pennsylvania. The director of the camp was Howie Garfinkel, who is quoted in Morgan's book as remarking, "He's dominating the league, killing everyone . . . It was obvious we were watching a star of the future."[2]

The camp was divided into underclassmen and seniors. After watching LeBron play for the underclassmen, Garfinkel wanted to move him to the senior group. LeBron, however, wanted to stay with his peers. To accommodate everyone, Garfinkel let James play in both groups, the first time any high school player had every done that. LeBron played so well that he was asked to play in both All-Star games. In the book, *King James: Believe the Hype: The LeBron James Story*, Ryan Jones quotes Garfinkel: "LeBron played as well or better than anyone of them [speaking of NBA players who had participated in the camp] when they were sophomores at my camp . . . he totally dominated. I've never seen anything like it."[3]

1 Quoted in David Lee Morgan. *LeBron James: The Rise of a Star.* Cleveland: Gray and Company, 2003, p. 77.
2 Quoted in Ryan Jones. *King James: Believe the Hype: The LeBron James Story.* New York: St. Martin's Press, 2003, p. 48.

attend the camps. LeBron headed first to Colorado Springs for the USA Basketball Development Festival. As the first underclassman ever to be invited, LeBron proved his worth by breaking the camp's scoring record. He accomplished this by scoring 120 points in five games. By camp's end, he had been voted the most valuable player.

From Colorado, LeBron traveled to New Jersey, where he played in the ABCD Camp. There, other well-known high school players took a back seat to the talented sophomore. Perhaps the best exposure for LeBron, however, came from attending Oakland, California's Slam-N-Jam. Initially, the sponsors of the Oakland camp refused to accept LeBron because, at fifteen, they claimed he was too young. With pressure from Dambrot and others, the organizers finally invited LeBron to attend. LeBron was placed on the lowest ranked of the Oakland teams, called Soldiers I. LeBron's performance there wowed even the skeptics, earning him a "graduation" into the higher level teams.

Because of his attendance at so many different camps, LeBron was able to meet and play with college and professional players as well as the best high school stars in the country. LeBron wrote about his trips to the summer camps for *SLAM* magazine in the form of a diary he kept throughout the summer season. He wrote: "It was cool. I got to run with a lot of the other NBA guys and I talked to [Michael] Jordan a little bit. He didn't really give me any advice. He just told me to keep my head on straight."[30]

Junior Year

After completing the summer season, LeBron was ready for his junior year. By that time, because of local media coverage of St. Vincent's games, he had become a well-known basketball name in Ohio. As his fame spread in the state, attendance at St. Vincent games steadily increased. The small St. Vincent gymnasium could no longer hold the large crowds that wanted to watch him play. As a result, the school decided to move most of its home games to the nearby and larger University of Akron Rhodes Arena. Many of the school's games were also shown on pay-per-view television in the Akron and Cleveland areas.

With Dambrot gone, LeBron and the other players were thrilled to learn that their former coach Dru Joyce II had been hired as the new St. Vincent coach. Looking at the season ahead, Joyce and his players knew in advance that the team would be facing some of their toughest opponents ever. Many of their games were against nationally ranked schools and they would be traveling across the country a number of times.

For the first time since LeBron had joined the Irish, the team lost two games in a row. The first loss was to a team that was fast becoming their number one rival—Oak Hill Academy. Despite LeBron scoring thirty-six points, the Irish lost the game. A few days later, this loss was followed by another one to George Junior Republic High School of Pennsylvania. LeBron commented on the losses: "Basically we played good and they played great. To tell you the truth, though, I think it made us better. It told us that we can be beat, that we have to turn up our intensity."[31] The team rebounded from the double losses to start a new winning streak.

Despite the earlier losses, LeBron had a great junior year in basketball. Praise from sports writers across the country began to pour in. Sports writer Scott Fowler wrote: "There is basketball. There is hype. And flying in midair between the two there is LeBron James, a . . . high school star who is so good and so well-publicized that it's impossible to tell where the hoops stop and the hype begins." After watching LeBron play, he added, "It was like watching Serena Williams serve it up for the high school girls' tennis team . . . James was strikingly better than everyone else on the court."[32]

LeBron finished his junior year with a twenty-eight point average, along with nine rebounds (catching the ball after a missed shot) a game, and was given his second Mr. Basketball award. He was also named to the all-USA first team in both *USA Today* and *People* magazine and received the 2001–2002 Gatorade National Boys Basketball Player of the Year award.

These awards, however, were overshadowed by St. Vincent's loss in the Ohio state title game to Cincinnati's Roger Bacon High School by a score of 71–63. It was their first loss to an Ohio team since LeBron had joined. LeBron commented on the loss: "Instead of me dwelling on this game, it's going to make me a lot hungrier to come back next year."[33]

By the end of the state finals, LeBron had already received invitations to play for several college basketball teams, all of whom assured LeBron that they would be offering him athletic scholarships. LeBron expressed interest in playing for several teams, including North Carolina, Duke, Ohio State, Michigan,

The St. Vincent basketball team, starring LeBron, became well known in Akron and attracted large crowds.

and Florida, but in his heart, he was already leaning towards going directly into the pros. Jones elaborates: "A year before he would make it official, LeBron acknowledged that it was unlikely he'd ever play college basketball."[34]

"The Chosen One"

Towards the end of the basketball season, LeBron received yet another honor. On February 18, 2002, his picture appeared on the cover of *Sports Illustrated*. Beside his photograph were the words

*LeBron was featured on the cover of **Sports Illustrated** while he was just a junior in high school.*

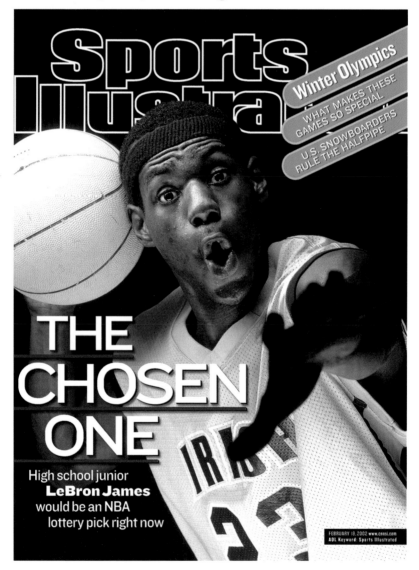

LeBron's Biggest Fan

Gloria James is, without doubt, LeBron's biggest fan and supporter. She attends almost every game he plays. By the time LeBron had reached high school, she was carrying cardboard cutouts of LeBron's face pasted on tongue depressors and passing them around to other fans in the stands. She nearly always wore a sweatshirt in the team's colors that had "LeBron's Mom" stenciled on the front. "Glo loved it all, loved greeting friends and fans with a hug, loved being recognized," author Ryan Jones elaborates in *King James: Believe the Hype: The LeBron James Story*, "and most of all, loved seeing her son succeed."[1]

Gloria was very vocal at LeBron's games and sometimes what critics called "over the top" in her support. During his junior year, for instance, she got into a shouting match with the mother and family of an opposing player. She occasionally taunted and antagonized the crowd at away games and was sometimes booed. Throughout it all, LeBron never let it bother him. In David Lee Morgan's book, *LeBron James: The Rise of a Star,* he quotes LeBron: "I know people think my mother is loud and stuff like that. But I love her to death."[2]

Gloria reveled in LeBron's star status, even the overwhelming pressure from the media. Jones quotes Gloria in *King James:* "The fans are great. The media—the majority of the media—is pretty considerate. Some of them . . . can be a little overpersistent sometimes. But all in all, the attention is good. We enjoy it, and we appreciate it, because without the fans, LeBron . . . is really nobody."[3]

1 Ryan Jones. *King James: Believe the Hype: The LeBron James Story*. New York: St. Martin's Press, 2003, p. 20.
2 Quoted in David Lee Morgan. *LeBron James: The Rise of a Star*. Cleveland: Gray and Company, 2003, p. 120.
3 Quoted in Jones. *King James*, p. 20.

"The Chosen One." Jones, in summarizing the importance of this coverage, wrote that it established "LeBron's status as the most publicized high school basketball player in at least a generation. . ."[35]

The accompanying article was written by Grant Wahl, one of the magazine's top sports writers. In the article, Wahl wrote that even as a junior in high school, James was ready for the National Basketball Association. NBA player and coach Danny Ainge agreed: "if I were a general manager, there are only four or five NBA players that I wouldn't trade to get him [LeBron] right now . . . If LeBron came out this year, I wouldn't even have to think about it. I'd take him number one." [36]

The magazine sold out in Akron the moment it hit the newsstands and bookstores. The article also introduced sports fans and readers outside Ohio to the basketball phenomenon. For the rest of his basketball career, thanks to the article and cover story, LeBron would be featured almost daily in both the *Cleveland Plain Dealer* and the *Akron Beacon Journal*. He also featured prominently on radio and television sports reporting in northeast Ohio and elsewhere.

"More Autographs than Mike"

After the *Sports Illustrated* article was released, LeBron attracted the attention of Cleveland Cavaliers coach John Lucas, who had been following LeBron's high school career. Lucas invited LeBron to practice with the professional team during the summer of 2002. Like other coaches before him, Lucas was amazed at the high school player's abilities and skills. However, his kind of contact with a high school player still in his junior year is not allowed by the NBA. As a result, Lucas was suspended for several games and the Cavaliers were fined $150,000.

Not long after the Cavaliers workout, LeBron broke his wrist. During a pick-up game he had been undercut by another player while in the air and landed heavily on his non-shooting hand. It was a scary incident but the star breathed a sigh of relief as he acknowledged that the fracture could have been much worse. A serious break, requiring surgery or long-term rehabiliation, could have jeopardized his future career. As it was, LeBron was out of action for a good part of the summer.

Despite not being able to play, LeBron went ahead and attended several summer camps, primarily for the contacts and experience. In mid-August of that summer, for instance, he attended Michael Jordan's basketball camp in California. Instead of playing, LeBron served as one of the counselors. While there, his cast came off and he was able to play briefly in a few casual games with NBA and college players. LeBron's friend Maverick Carter also attended. He commented, "He [LeBron] signed more autographs than Mike [Jordan]."[37]

Chapter 3

Believe the Hype

As he entered his senior year in high school, even though his broken wrist had healed, LeBron chose not to play football. He told his friends and family that he wanted to concentrate solely on basketball. By this time, LeBron had grown to his present height of 6 feet 8 inches (2m 3cm) tall. His basketball skills were at a remarkable level. Former college and NBA all-star Austin Carr commented,

> You could see he was the real deal in high school. First of all, physically he was much bigger than everybody else . . . And his understanding of the game was remarkable. LeBron could have averaged fifty points a game . . . if he wanted to but, because of his knowledge of the game and knowing that he couldn't do it by himself, he chose to do it another way. And that showed me a lot of discipline and restraint, because at the high school level, it's all about 'me, me, me' and LeBron was never that way.[38]

While LeBron had been approached by a number of colleges during his junior year, by the start of his senior year he had already made his decision. He would go directly to the NBA. Although no formal announcement had been made, the media had already surmised as much. Even before the basketball season began, the majority of sports writers were predicting that LeBron would be the top draft pick in June 2003. Biographer Ryan Jones comments on the excitement and hype that surrounded James:

> Barring serious injury or a total collapse of his game, LeBron's massive payday was less than a year away; the catch was that

while amateur ideals technically prevented him from making so much as a penny off his talent, he was already being treated as a millionaire.[39]

From the beginning of the year, the media put constant demands on LeBron, while potential agents hovered around his family, making promises of fame and fortune. LeBron, rather than knuckle under to all the pressure, decided that there was only one thing he could do to make it through the year—enjoy the media attention and play his game. In fact, the more pressure that surrounded him, the better LeBron seemed to do. He thrived on the challenges, and during his senior year had plenty of those to contend with.

"This Young Man Has Been Totally Exploited"

One of the first questions that arose during LeBron's final high school season was whether he was being exploited. Many sports analysts and school officials all over the country blamed LeBron's high school for taking advantage of the young star's talents for financial reasons. The school's decision to move their games to nearby Akron University in order to seat more fans was criticized along with the pay-per-view television coverage of LeBron's games. It was reported, for instance, that St. Vincent–St. Mary had made nearly $250,000 during LeBron's junior year as a result of the team's out-of-town appearances and ticket sales. Sports writer Kaufman elaborates: "Critics say James's school is doing him a disservice and tainting the purity of amateur athletics by moving games to a bigger venue and raising ticket prices."[40]

Ohio High School Athletic Association Commissioner (OHSAA) Clair Muscaro had also been keeping an eye on LeBron and his high school. OHSAA, like other state sports associations, was responsible for assuring that high school athletics remain untainted by any non-amateur behavior or financial gain. Muscaro, as head of OHSAA, firmly believed that the young man was being exploited. He stated: "This young man has been totally exploited. The

OHSAA Commissioner Clair Muscaro, like many others, felt that LeBron was being exploited.

pay-per-view television, the amount schools are charging for games, I think it's just ridiculous."[41] Sports writer Michael Rand agreed and commented: "With our morals neatly folded into wallets, anything that draws crowds seems to be fair game."[42]

Bob Hughes, the commissioner of the Florida High School Athletic Association also weighed in on the controversy. He stated:

> The purpose of high school athletics is not to get publicity for one outstanding student or to accommodate outsiders who want to cash in on that student. The purpose of high school sports is to offer a rewarding, enriching experience to

all students and showcase all athletes, not just those bound for the NBA, NFL, or the PGA.[43]

Athletic association officials were not the only ones to comment on the issue. One of the most vocal critics was former basketball player and current college analyst Billy Packer, who stated:

> To take a high school player and overhype him the way he has been is ridiculous. I think it's disgusting. It's part of the problem that has evolved in all sports, but particularly in basketball—making people something before they actually are something. This kid may become the greatest player who has ever played the game, but let's let him do that.[44]

"Sometimes It Got to Be Too Much"

Instead of blaming LeBron's school, other analysts and sports officials criticized the media for his exploitation. Grant Innocenzi, the athletic director at St. Vincent–St. Mary High School, accused the media, stating that most of the controversy "was generated by the media. Once LeBron was in *Sports Illustrated*, things got crazy."[45] The school took firm steps to keep the media from doing further damage by blocking media access to the school and requiring that all interviews be preapproved by LeBron, his mother, his coach, or Eddie Jackson.

Among those accused of taking advantage of the young man were the hundreds of people hoping to make a profit from LeBron. Clothing companies, shoe executives, and others flocked to his side with million-dollar offers if LeBron would sign with them at the end of his senior year. In addition to the advertising world, others also wanted to make money by selling LeBron James items on eBay and elsewhere. An autographed copy of his *Sports Illustrated* cover story sold for $77, while a signed basketball went for $112.50. Everyone wanted a piece of LeBron, as Bill Livingston of the *Cleveland Plain Dealer* remarked: "All of America's money-driven, celebrity-mad, sell-at-any-price, get-a-life exploitive sports culture has descended on the kid."[46]

The media attention took an emotional toll on LeBron. It stripped away any sense of normalcy in his life. The only places that he felt safe from the onslaught were at home and at school. He commented on the pressure: "Sometimes it got to be too much. Sometimes I would wake up and I didn't want to go to

Demands for LeBron's Time

As a high school senior, LeBron was bombarded with demands for his time. He was forced to turn down many requests, however, including invitations to appear on a number of television shows. Regis Philbin wanted to shoot hoops with him, while David Letterman wanted to interview him. These requests were denied. "We said no because what his mom really wants him to do is just play basketball now,"[1] said Chris Dennis, a family friend and spokesperson, quoted in "Sky-High Schooler" in the *Denver Rocky Mountain News*.

LeBron did respond personally to many of the thousands of letters that were sent to him. In particular, he usually wrote back to the youngsters who contacted him. LeBron even received a T-shirt with Valencia, Spain, on it. The T-shirt came from a sixteen-year-old Spanish youngster who asked LeBron to sign it and return it to her. He did so with pleasure. On the other hand, a request from a woman in Akron for LeBron to come to her husband's birthday party was declined.

Another example of his generosity came as a result of a fire that LeBron read about in the Akron paper. Demitra Greer had lost three family members in a fire, but her son, nine-year-old Davonte, had survived. After hearing of the family's tragedy, LeBron invited Davonte to one of his games. The boy told everyone how thrilled he had been to be included in the St. Vincent huddle when the introductions were made.

1 Quoted in Chris Tomasson. "Sky-High Schooler." *Denver Rocky Mountain News,* January 4, 2003.

school at all because it drained me a lot."[47] But in spite of the demands on his time and attention, LeBron managed to keep up his good grades and maintained good relationships with his classmates and teachers. When asked if he felt exploited, LeBron responded, "I don't know. You tell me. I'm just going out there playing my game. Y'all are making all the remarks."[48] The media and others deny the charges of exploitation, claiming that LeBron is "a once-in-a-generation player with talent to match the attention he's getting."[49]

Despite all the pressure, LeBron held up well. "Without exception," writes Jones, "the hotter the spotlight has gotten, the more impressively LeBron has performed. Of those intangibles . . . this ability to rise to the moment is his most defining."[50]

"I'm Going to Put on a Show"

Because of all the media attention, American sports fans had been reading about LeBron for more than a year, but most had never seen him play. That changed on December 12, 2002, when fans had the chance to see if what the media had been claiming was true. Sports network ESPN 2 had announced that for the first time they would televise a high school basketball game. As fans across the country tuned in that night, they were told that there was a sellout crowd at Cleveland State University Convocation Center to watch the much-publicized high school teenager play basketball. The game would give LeBron a chance to showcase his talents to sports fans across the country.

On hand to broadcast the game was Dick Vitale, the voice of college basketball and an enthusiastic expert on everything related to the sport. Beside Vitale sat former NBA star and Hall-of-Famer Bill Walton, a long-time professional basketball announcer. Both broadcasters expressed excitement during the pregame show, telling viewers how anxious they were to have this opportunity to watch LeBron play. The broadcast was one of the top-rated shows in the network's history.

The opponent for St. Vincent–St. Mary that night in December was their rival, Oak Hill Academy of Virginia. Oak Hill was a powerhouse team nationally known for its excellent players and

LeBron put on a show for the country at the St. Vincent–Oak Hill game televised by ESPN on December 12, 2002.

winning record. St. Vincent had played Oak Hill twice since LeBron had joined the team and had lost both previous encounters. Both teams were coming into the game with perfect records. The stage was set for an evening of high school basketball at its best. Oak Hill's team that year was led by all-star player Carmelo Anthony. The following year, Anthony would help Syracuse University win the national college championship and eventually he would go on to play for the Denver Nuggets. He and LeBron would also become good friends.

Interviewed before the game, LeBron told reporters: "I can't wait for the game. I'm going to put on a show." [51] LeBron's words came true. He ended up scoring thirty-one points and had thirteen rebounds and six assists (passes to teammates that resulted in a score.) St. Vincent beat Oak Hill by a score of 65–45. Sports writer Marty Burns was on hand for the game and reported:

> With scouts from about a dozen NBA teams on hand along with some one hundred media members, James showed why he's widely considered the likely first overall pick in next June's NBA draft . . . He made big shots. He crashed the boards. He hit the open man . . . Once he caught the ball on the wing and started to make a move but stopped when he saw the double team. Instead of trying to force it, he calmly stepped back to create space, spotted an open teammate and then rifled a perfect cross-court skip-pass over the defense. It was a play you often see in the NBA, but rarely in a high school game.[52]

LeBron had proven that he was, indeed, worthy of all the praise that was being heaped on him.

The Hummer Controversy

Following the Oak Hill victory, St. Vincent won the rest of their games in December and then took time off for the holidays. Expectations were high that the school would go undefeated for the remainder of the year. However, controversy soon developed and it centered around the school's star player, LeBron James.

On January 10, 2003, the *Cleveland Plain Dealer* wrote a story about LeBron driving a brand-new platinum/silver Hummer SUV that had a DVD player, three televisions, a Play Station 2, and a leather interior. Questions immediately arose about how a poor family like LeBron's could afford such an expensive car. Rumors began to circulate that the car was a gift from one of the shoe and equipment companies who were interested in LeBron.

The Ohio High School Athletic Association carried out an immediate investigation, led by Commissioner Clair Muscaro. The question was whether the car purchase somehow violated the rules on amateur athletics that do not allow high school players from benefiting financially or materially during their amateur careers. After a three-week investigation, however, the matter was dropped and LeBron was cleared of all responsibility and blame. In a statement to the press, Muscaro announced: "I was satisfied with the documentation that we were given . . . I am satisfied that the loan that was granted did not violate our guidelines and was acquired by his mother." [53]

LeBron's mother Gloria, it was learned, had taken out a loan to buy the car based on LeBron's future potential earning power. Gloria admitted that the purchase was probably bad timing but that she and Eddie had investigated the matter thoroughly before buying the car. "We checked with everybody we needed before the vehicle was purchased," Eddie stated, "to make sure LeBron's eligibility wouldn't be jeopardized." [54]

The Jersey Scandal

Just days after the Hummer incident had been resolved, LeBron and his teammates traveled to Cleveland. While there, they went to Next Urban Gear, a popular store that sold jerseys and other sports items. LeBron and other high school students were big fans of what are referred to as "throwback" jerseys. These are jerseys bearing the names and numbers of noted athletes in every sport, and they can retail for hundreds of dollars. While in the store, LeBron was approached by the store manager, Joe Hathorn, who gave LeBron two throwback jerseys valued at $845. The jerseys bore the names of Gale Sayers, of Chicago Bears football fame, and Wes Unseld, a well-known NBA player.

Not long after the store visit, the Ohio High School Athletic Association learned of the gifts and announced that LeBron would be suspended for violating their bylaws. OHSAA Commissioner Clair Muscaro announced: "In talking with the store's personnel, I was able to confirm that on January 25, the merchant gave the clothing directly to LeBron at no cost. Accordingly, this is a direct violation of the OHSAA bylaws on amateurism because LeBron did capitalize on athletic fame by receiving these gifts." [55] Muscaro also announced that St. Vincent–St. Mary would have to forfeit its last victory. The biggest news, however, was that LeBron James's high school career appeared to be over.

The throwback jerseys of football great Gale Sayers and NBA player Wes Unseld ignited a controversy that threatened to end LeBron's career.

Immediately after Muscaro's announcement on January 30, 2003, LeBron's mother Gloria contacted Cleveland lawyer Fred Nance to intervene on her son's behalf. Gloria was incensed, claiming that Muscaro never even talked to LeBron, or notified the family of the suspension, until it was publicized in the news. She stated: "None of us was even notified by OHSAA that an investigation was under way, much less permitted to provide any information. We do not understand how this could be considered a fair process."[56] School officials at St. Vincent also weighed in with criticism: "LeBron did nothing that would justify the decision by the OHSAA to suspend his eligibility . . . The consequences are so severe, it's far disproportionate to the conduct . . . As part of our school community, he deserves our wholehearted support."[57]

Senior Night

As LeBron's senior year came to an end, St. Vincent held its annual Senior Night at the Irish's last home game. The night was used to acknowledge all the senior basketball players on the team, along with their families. LeBron had been looking forward to the occasion as an opportunity to recognize his mother, along with Eddie Jackson, for everything they had done for him.

When the night arrived, however, both Gloria and Eddie were elsewhere. Eddie was in jail, convicted of mail and bank fraud. Gloria, on the other hand, was in court dealing with financial problems that had resulted from an accident LeBron had in his Hummer. She told LeBron that she would do her best to be there but could not guarantee she would make it. When she failed to appear, most reporters just assumed she was out partying.

With neither Gloria nor Eddie present, LeBron waited alone by the sidelines for his name to be announced. High school officials delayed the ceremony to give his mother ample time to appear, but at last they had to proceed with the evening. His teammates and friends were announced first and walked proudly to center court with their parents. Then it was LeBron's turn and his name was called. As he walked forward, his friends left their parents and made their way towards LeBron. They encircled him with their arms and together walked to center court. In *LeBron James: The Rise of a Star* David Lee Morgan describes how LeBron, in speaking to the crowd, stated: "Today was a special day for me and my teammates . . . We grew up together, did a lot of things together . . ."[1]

LeBron matured into a real team player at St. Vincent.

1 Quoted in David Lee Morgan. *LeBron James: The Rise of a Star.* Cleveland: Gray and Company, 2003, p. 150.

During his high school career, LeBron received many honors, including his jersey going to the Naismith Basketball Hall of Fame.

The criticisms proved to have merit, for when attorney Nance investigated, he was told that the store owner gave LeBron the jerseys because of academic excellence, not athletic abilities. After much legal hassle, including an injunction against OHSAA that enabled LeBron to play, the matter was resolved to LeBron's benefit. The school ended up forfeiting one victory, while LeBron missed two games, but he was then allowed to return to the basketball court.

As the controversy passed, blame was placed on the media who had aired the story daily for several days. The Cleveland papers that had broken the story were criticized by Ohio basketball fans, while its reporters actually received death threats. As Jones explains: ". . . a media assault . . . turned one talented high school athlete's brief lapse of judgment into a nationally broadcast scandal."[58] Many sports writers argued that LeBron, because of the Hummer incident, must have understood the amateur rules about accepting gifts. They wrote that LeBron should never have accepted the jerseys, regardless of the intent of the store owner.

LeBron played down the incident by stating, "Adversity was nothing new to me. Blaming other people is the easy way out. I blame myself . . . it made me a better person. It made me stronger."[59] He proved his point by scoring more than fifty points in his first game on the court after the suspension.

"I Played for Myself and the Team"

Despite the scandals and the pressure from the media and elsewhere, LeBron finished the season playing some of his best basketball. During the last months of the basketball season, his team played some of the best teams in the country. In Los Angeles, St. Vincent played Mater Dei of Santa Ana, the number four–ranked team in the country, and won 64–58; LeBron scored twenty-one points. In New Jersey, they played Los Angeles West Chester and won 78–57, with LeBron scoring a career-high fifty-two points. "I didn't play for the crowd. I played for myself and the team," LeBron told reporters. "I loved the adversity because every night we came out and we knew that we were going to get our opponent's best game."[60]

The Irish went undefeated for the rest of the year and were called one of the best teams in Ohio high school history. The team also went to the state championship as a solid favorite. Despite their one loss, they were ranked number one in the nation by *USA Today*. In front of a sellout crowd in Columbus, Ohio, St. Vincent had a slight lead going into the fourth quarter of the championship game against Kettering Alter High School. A sports Web site reported what happened next: "That's when LeBron took over—he scored his team's first nine points of the final stanza to spark St. Vincent–St. Mary to a 40–36 victory."[61] In beating Kettering Alter High School, the team won their third championship in four years and finished the 2002–2003 season with a 24–1 record.

Afterwards, LeBron was awarded his third straight Mr. Basketball award, which was something that no other player had ever achieved. It was also announced that one of LeBron's high school jerseys was going to the Naismith Basketball Hall of Fame, an unusual honor for a high school player.

Other accolades poured in from all over the basketball world. David Lumpkin of Cincinnati's Winton Woods High School stated:

> He's phenomenal . . . I've seen very few kids in high school who come close to doing what he can do. He can score anytime he wants to. He could average fifty a game in high school if he wanted to, but he prides himself on being an all-around player. I've never seen anything like him.[62]

The All-Star Games

In late April and May 2003, after the championship game was over, LeBron was invited to play in several important high school All-Star games. These games are a critical part of a senior's high school season, and they are the best way to showcase their talents before entering college or the NBA.

Giving Back

During LeBron's senior year in high school, he decided to do something special for those Akron youngsters who were facing many of the same obstacles he had faced when growing up. Because Elizabeth Park had been such a special place for LeBron and his mother, LeBron decided to focus his attention there. LeBron and his family contacted businesses in the Elizabeth Park area, asking for donations of school supplies and other items. In David Lee Morgan's book, *LeBron James: The Rise of a Star*, family friend Chris Dennis explains: "His mother and Eddie were always trying to help out people in the community, as far as donating things to the recreation centers, especially at Elizabeth Park. So LeBron wanted to start doing the same."[1]

LeBron was able to persuade Nike and Adidas to donate sports gear for the youngsters. Delivering the items to an Elizabeth Park gymnasium, LeBron stayed to meet the kids and gave everyone a "high five". He also handed out bookmarks to children at the Akron Community Service Center and Urban League. Morgan writes about how LeBron was particularly proud of the bookmark, for it contained one of his own quotes: "My achievements in basketball have made me famous, but if I didn't do the work in the classroom, you would never know who I am."[2]

LeBron told the press that he took the job of being a role model seriously. He had experienced the benefit that such role models brought to his own life and he wanted to do the same for others. He relished the knowledge that he could use his stardom to do good things for younger children and perhaps make a difference in their lives.

1 Quoted in David Lee Morgan. *LeBron James: The Rise of a Star.* Cleveland: Gray and Company, 2003, p.111.
2 Quoted in Morgan. *LeBron James: The Rise of a Star*, p. 111.

Perhaps the biggest and best known of these games is the McDonald's High School All-American game; an event that has produced fifteen top overall draft picks for the NBA. The 2003

McDonald's game was played at Gund Arena in Cleveland. The seats were filled with thousands of LeBron's fans. Biographer Jones writes about the game: "Even on a court filled with the best 18-year-olds in the nation, LeBron once again stood out from the crowd."[63] LeBron's team won 122–107, while LeBron himself made over 50 percent of his shots and won the John Wooden Award as the most valuable player. One NBA scout was overheard saying, "He's on a different level from these kids."[64]

LeBron also played in the 39th Annual Roundball Classic, scoring twenty-eight points and receiving the Most Valuable Player award, while leading his team to a 120-119 victory. His final amateur game was the Jordan Brand Capital Classic, which is held annually in Washington, D. C. By appearing in this game, LeBron ended any question about whether he was going to go to college or turn professional. A graduating senior who is college-bound is only allowed to play in two post-season games; by appearing in three, LeBron made it clear that he was going to the NBA. While LeBron's team lost in the Jordan Classic, his sterling play earned him yet another Most Valuable Player award.

After the all-star games were over, LeBron still had thirty days of school left before he graduated in early June. Athletic equipment companies were beginning to swarm around the young man as he contemplated his future. He was about to become very rich. All of his hard work, together with all of Gloria's support, were about to pay off.

Chapter 4

Rookie Sensation

Not long after the completion of the All-Star games, LeBron James officially announced that he would be entering the June 2003 NBA draft. Speculation arose immediately over which professional team would take him. He was assumed by everyone to be the front runner for the number-one draft choice. Sports writer Michelle Kaufman talked about why James would be chosen first:

> Without question, LeBron is the best player in the draft, the kind of player who comes around once every fifteen years. . . He is so versatile . . . and he's not a good kid, he's a great kid. A marketing dream. He's the whole package and he'll be worth every penny someone pays for him.[65]

LeBron Becomes a Multimillionaire

Meanwhile, as James and the sports world waited for the draft to take place, he was bombarded by shoe and athletic company executives. The companies were competing for James to sign profitable endorsements. As his graduation day approached, Nike, Reebok, and Adidas—the "big three" in shoe sales—increased the pressure. All three companies flew James and his mother to their headquarters, offering them first-class hotel rooms and enticing them with rich offers. Such offers were normal in sports, as Morgan explains: "Professional sports is about selling merchandise."[66] Many of the shoes that are endorsed by professional athletes, for instance, sell for as much as $200 a pair, earning enormous profits for the manufacturers.

LeBron—The Millionaire

Shortly after signing a huge deal with Nike, LeBron James made a number of other endorsements that brought his total assets to $143 million. One of the most profitable deals was with Bubblicious Bubble Gum, with whom he signed a four-year contract for $5 million. This was a natural for James since he had been chewing their gum throughout his high school career. Today, he even has his own flavor of Bubblicious gum called "LeBron's Lightning Lemonade."

James also signed a deal with Upper Deck Trading Cards for four years and $7 million. Buyers of the trading cards had the opportunity to buy a one-of-a-kind collectible card that included a photograph of LeBron James and Michael Jordan. The card also contained material from their jerseys; a single card sold for as much as $1,000 on eBay.

James has also been visible on television doing commercials for Coca-Cola and their products. In one advertisement that was aired during his rookie season, James appeared on the basketball court where he was shooting baskets from impossible distances. Despite his prowess with a basketball, these eighty-foot shots were made using special computer effects. Coca-Cola paid the star nearly $20 million for being their spokesperson.

James has also appeared in a running commercial that stars a family called the LeBrons. During the advertisement, James plays all the characters in the scene. He has also appeared as himself on an episode of *The Simpsons*. The television appearances have brought James more exposure. Today, he is one of the highest-paid sports stars.

Upper Deck Trading Cards created a collectible card of LeBron and Michael Jordan.

The first LeBron James signature shoe was the Nike Air Zoom Generation.

When the time came to finalize a deal, James chose Nike. He signed an endorsement with them for more than $90 million. Sports writer Tom Withers writes about the day James signed the contract: "LeBron went to school Thursday with enough lunch money for everyone. The hyped high school player . . . [had just] signed a multiyear endorsement deal with Nike . . ."[67] After signing the seven-year deal, James commented, "Nike is the right fit and has the right product for me. They are a great group of people who are committed to supporting me throughout my professional career, on and off the court."[68] The deal was the most expensive endorsement ever given to a player who had never played in professional sports.

The first LeBron James signature shoe, the "Air Zoom Generation," came out within weeks of the deal and sold out in shoe stores throughout the country. It was partly modeled after James's Hummer sports vehicle. Nike also began production of a line of personal apparel (clothing) for James. In 2005, Nike improved on the James shoe and unveiled a new and better version of his "King James" line. It has been reported that more than one thousand people at *Nike* are involved in the production and marketing of the James apparel and shoes.

Number One Pick

With the *Nike* and other endorsement deals signed, sealed, and delivered, James's attention turned to the upcoming draft. The media was also closely following the developments. All eyes in the sports world tuned in on May 22, 2003, the night the draft lottery was held.

The team with the best chance of signing James was the Cleveland Cavaliers, a squad desperately in need of a superstar. In order to gain the first draft choice, the team would first have to win the NBA lottery. The lottery is held each year and involves the teams with the worst records in the league. A ping-pong ball could make the difference of a winning or losing season.

As the representatives from the NBA teams watched, ping-pong balls were drawn from a rotating machine by an NBA representative to determine the order of the draft. Those teams with the worst losing seasons had the best chance to win the first choice. The lottery is a complicated procedure in which fourteen balls, numbered one to fourteen, are placed in the machine. Four balls are drawn at a time and the combination of the four numbers decides the order of the draft for the fourteen teams not in the playoffs. The teams are ranked from one to fourteen, with number one being the team with the worst record. That team has a 25 percent chance of getting the first pick; 250 different combinations of the four balls will cause this result. The fourteenth-ranked team has a 0.5 percent chance of winning the first pick; only five winning combinations will cause this result. After each turn, all the balls are returned to the container and the next four balls determine the next choice. The number-one draft pick is selected last. After all the other balls had been selected, only two teams remained—the Cleveland Cavaliers and the Memphis Grizzlies. All over Cleveland and northwest Ohio, people held their breaths as they watched the televised show. Cheers erupted all over the

Accompanied by the cheers of thousands, LeBron James was drafted by the Cleveland Cavaliers in 2003.

area when Memphis was selected to take the number-two choice. That left Cleveland with number one—and LeBron James.

If any city was in need of a star player, it was Cleveland. The last time the city had had a professional team at a championship in any sport was in 1964 when the Cleveland Browns won the

NFL championship. Cleveland sports fans had struggled through losing season after losing season.

The Cleveland Cavaliers, in particular, had always been somewhat of a mockery. The basketball team had lost sixty-five out of its eighty-two games in 2002–2003. Thus, when the team won the right to have the first pick, people in the bars and other places in Cleveland and Akron broke into wild celebrations. Rick Noland, a sports writer who has covered the Cavaliers for years, talked of how big the night had been: "That night was, by far, the biggest night in franchise history." [69]

It was assumed that the Cavaliers would pick James. People celebrated like the team had just won a championship. Immediately after the announcement, ticket sales at Gund Arena increased dramatically. Team owner Gordon Gund spoke of the importance of getting the first pick: "We really needed a pickup, and we couldn't have asked for a better one." [70]

The Cavaliers finally made it official on June 6, 2003, when NBA Commissioner David Stern made the announcement that James had been selected by Cleveland. When interviewed after the announcement, James told reporters, "Ya'll come to Cleveland. It'll be lit up like Vegas." [71]

High Expectations

With the draft completed, the expectations on James rose to phenomenal levels. James knew the odds were stacked against him. Only about one in ten thousand high school players ever make it to the professional level, much less become a superstar. James knew that the media and fans expected him to make the Cavaliers a play-off team, but he was also realistic. Early in the season James proclaimed: "Expectations are real high for me. I'm supposed to score fifty points each night to keep everyone happy . . . I ain't the savior of the NBA." [72]

James also told reporters that he didn't want to always be in the spotlight or take any credit away from his teammates. "I don't want to be a cocky rookie," James said. "I'm going to lead by example this first year. If there's one message I want to get to my teammates, it's that I'll be there for them, do whatever they think I need to do."[73]

Staying out of the limelight, however, proved difficult to accomplish. Even before James signed with the Cavaliers, the media was following the young star everywhere he went. Reporters surrounded James after each workout and game. Cavalier coach Paul Silas summarized: "It was before the draft, and he had come in for a workout. So the two of us are out there on the floor, and then I turn around and there are literally one hundred media people watching us go through all of this."[74]

Sports Illustrated reporter Jack McCallum agreed with Silas and commented on the media frenzy: "No one has gotten this much this soon; no one has ever entered any league under so much scrutiny."[75] A few people in the media, like McCallum, acknowledged that the pressure was high. One biographer elaborates: "The lights glared, the expectations rose and the pressure intensified in LeBron's first season with the Cavs. Of course, he had been performing under similar conditions most of his life."[76]

Despite the high expectations, James's maturity showed through as he remained focused when he took the court. Asked repeatedly if he could deal with the media pressure, James stated, "I can handle it."[77] But he also acknowledged that the personal price of this fame was high. "It's going to be a stir no matter where I go," James stated. "I go to the movies and I go out for shopping and if people want autographs, sometimes I just try to finish my shopping before I do that."[78]

"He Was Ready for the Pros"

With media and fan interest high, James took the court for his first regular season professional game in Sacramento against the Kings. At age eighteen, he was the youngest player on the floor. In the starting lineup, he played like a veteran. It was quickly obvious to the media and fans that he was the best Cavalier on the floor.

While the Cavaliers lost the game, James played well, scoring twenty-five points, getting six rebounds, nine assists, and four steals. Author Roger Gordon reports on James's performance:

The LeBron James bobblehead was one of the few made to honor a rookie.

. . . [In] his first game as a professional . . . he shocked the basketball world with a remarkable performance against a very good Kings team . . . the 6'8", 240-pound, LeBron James proved time and again that four years of college ball would have done nothing but delay his NBA fame and fortune. He was ready for the pros—more than ready.[79]

After a brief road schedule, the Cavaliers returned to Cleveland for a series of home games at Gund Arena. Before James's signing, the team could barely give away tickets for their games. On opening night of their first home stand, however, more than twenty thousand fans saw James play. Sportswriter Arana Lynch described the atmosphere: "James has brought a new attitude this city needs. It does not matter how many games the Cavaliers win or lose, as long as the city continues to win . . . James has put Cleveland on the map the way [Michael] Jordan did for Chicago."[80]

"From Another Planet"

By the end of the first few games, James's teamwork and solid play had won the respect and admiration of his coaches and teammates alike. James's goal, from the time he began playing the game, had always been to make his teammates better. He accomplished this at the professional level after just a few games. Coach Silas reported: "I think he goes out of his way to include the others. He wants them all to know that they're a part of this team. Early on he went out of his way to make sure they were comfortable with him."[81]

This trait of wanting to include his teammates pleased James's former coach and mentor Dru Joyce II. Joyce commented: "He's never really been a prima donna. As great as he's played this year with the Cavs, I'm even more proud of how he's handled himself and worked to blend in with his teammates."[82]

Perhaps the greatest strength, however, that LeBron brought to the Cavaliers was his court awareness. Biographer Roger Gordon elaborates: "James has the uncanny knack of seeing the action in slow motion or being one play or pass ahead of the others . . . There were times when it appeared that James was from another planet in terms of his court awareness."[83] James had always been gifted in finding open players on the court and he utilized this gift to increase his assists per game.

Most analysts agree that James adjusted to professional basketball quickly. "LeBron James isn't the first high schooler to jump to

From his first game with the Cavaliers, James proved why he was the first draft pick.

Comparisons to Other Players

Even before entering the NBA, LeBron James was already being compared to some of the best professional basketball players who had ever competed. Those comparisons increased in James's first few seasons as a professional. As Ryan Jones summarizes in *King James: Believe the Hype: The LeBron James Story:* "Fittingly, LeBron James was already being measured against some of the game's all-time greats."[1] Names like basketball superstars Kobe Bryant, Michael Jordan, Vince Carter, and Earvin "Magic" Johnson were being mentioned in the same breath as James by sports writers across the country.

Kobe Bryant was a common comparison since Bryant had also gone directly to the pros from high school. Many analysts who have seen both of them play say that James is better. James has also been compared to Magic Johnson, former Michigan State University and Los Angeles Lakers superstar. Many compare James's passing skills to those of Johnson.

In an article in the *Knight Ridder/Tribune News Service* by Kevin Horrigan, Bill Livingston of the *Cleveland Plain Dealer* is quoted: "He's the best high school player I've ever seen. He jumps like Jordan, he passes like Magic Johnson. He did one of those under-the-legs 360-degree tomahawk dunks like Vince Carter does, only he did it in a game."[2]

1 Ryan Jones. *King James: Believe the Hype: The LeBron James Story.* New York: St. Martin's Press, 2003, p. 59.
2 Quoted in Kevin Horrigan. "Deposed LeBron James a Commodity at Very Young Age." *Knight Ridder/Tribune News Service,* January 31, 2003.

the NBA, but he may be the best," wrote one sports website. "He already possesses the body and skills of an All-Star, and a basketball IQ that is nothing short of astonishing."[84] Tracy McGrady, one of professional basketball's superstars, also praised James: "He's unbelievable, incredible really . . . The pose that he has on the basketball court . . . He has that swagger, nothing rattles him at all. He's got extremely high confidence and he's a real competitor. At the age of 19, that's scary."[85]

Rookie of the Year

James's game continued to improve as the season progressed. Although not named to the All-Star team, James was invited to participate in the Rookie Challenge during All-Star weekend. A traditional part of the festivities is for the rookies to play the sophomores. Despite a thirty-three point performance, James and the rookie squad lost to the sophomores. His play, however, won him even more praise from the sports world.

James was also credited with turning around the Cavaliers record that year. Largely as a result of James's play, the Cavaliers improved their record to 35–47. This compared favorably to the team's record of 17–65 the previous year. A sports Web site elaborated on James's importance: "LeBron was the number-one reason for the team's turnaround . . . A team player from the opening training camp . . . he helped lift Cleveland from cellar-dweller to playoff contender."[86]

Before the season started, the majority of professional scouts and basketball analysts had predicted that James would probably average around ten to fifteen points a game during his rookie year, a figure that previous rookies had established. James exceeded all their expectations and predictions, ending up as one of the top fifteen scorers in the league. James averaged 20.9 points a game and was named NBA Rookie of the Year. He became the first Cavalier in franchise history and the youngest player in NBA history to earn this honor. He received seventy-eight out of a possible 118 first-place votes.

James was also one of the most popular players in the NBA during his rookie year. He was always a crowd favorite and never failed to sign autographs for children after the games. "LeBron has that special something, a combination of charisma and charm that makes people smile. He knows how to work a crowd."[87] James was humble in acknowledging this: "I just want to be myself. Pretty much, I think the crowds like me. It's good to see the smiles on young people's faces."[88]

James was the first Cavalier to play on an Olympic team.

Towards the end of his rookie year, James was selected for the 2004 men's Olympic basketball team. At age nineteen, he was the youngest player on the team and the first Cavalier ever to play on an Olympic team. James, on being chosen for the team, stated, "It's a dream come true for me to represent my country."[89] Despite his skills, however, he saw little action as coach Larry Brown chose to go with the more veteran players. James did not complain, as one Web site elaborates: "He displayed the type of dignity and class that veterans twice his age are known for. While . . . [others] were complaining about . . . lack of playing time, he kept quiet and did whatever coach Larry Brown asked of him."[90] The team finished in third place and came home with the bronze medal.

Impact on the Cavaliers

In addition to improving the Cavaliers overall record, James's presence meant more national exposure for the team. During the year before James joined the team, the Cavaliers had not appeared on television at all. During his rookie season, the Cavaliers were on television thirteen times. The team also sold out more than thirty away games in 2003–2004, compared to only six the previous year. Movie stars, rap singers, and other athletes frequently came to watch James play.

People came from miles away to watch James play. One family came all the way from Italy to see the superstar. When the Cavalier front desk learned of the family's long journey, they rolled out the red carpet. In addition to upgrading the group's tickets to front-row seats, they invited the Italian family down to the bench during warm-ups, where they were introduced to James. He signed multiple autographs for the entire group.

Because of this popularity, on March 3, 2004, the Cavaliers sponsored a LeBron James Bobblehead night. Bobbleheads, 6-to-12-inch figurines (15–30cm) with large moveable bobbing heads, have become increasingly popular among sports fans, but few rookies have been so honored. Fans in Cleveland lined up hours before the game in order to receive one of the ten thousand dolls

The Global Challenge

In late 2006, the NBA announced that several NBA stars would participate in summer basketball camps throughout the country. On ESPN.com in an article by Tom Farrey, spokesperson George Raveling describes the purpose: "It affords young people the chance to sit at the knees of the very best players and hear authentic stories on how they built their games and their careers."[1]

NBA stars Kobe Bryant, Steve Nash, Amare Stoudemire, Vince Carter, and LeBron James all participated in the camps. For four days, the kids learned from James, who himself learned to play from his own mentors. James has repeatedly spoken of his eagerness to impart his basketball knowledge to young people.

One of the biggest features of the 2007 summer program was the creation of a new international tournament called the Global Challenge. Held at the end of summer, the players of each region were invited to compete against teams from around the world.

James has already appeared in Tokyo, Beijing, and Hong Kong. PR Newswire quotes James: "I'm very excited about going to Asia. I've heard a lot of great things about the basketball culture in Asia and I can't wait to meet the kids, and inspire them with my style of play, and be inspired by them."[2]

1 Quoted in Tom Farrey. "LeBron, Nash Among Stars to Run Nike Summer Camps." *ESPN. com*, November 9, 2006. http://sports.espn.go.com/nba/news/story?id=2655836
2 Quoted in PR Newswire. "Nike Announces LeBron James Asia Tour Summer 2005." *PR Newswire*, July 8, 2005.

that were being given away. Gordon elaborates on this fan frenzy: "Fans would do just about anything to get a piece of LeBron James. Thousands throughout the season waited—sometimes in polar temperatures at all hours of the night—outside hotels in NBA cities across the country waiting to get a glimpse, take a picture of, cop an autograph, from the young star."[91]

In addition to his popularity with fans, James's presence in Cleveland also led to the growth of the downtown area. Many

James coaches kids at summer basketball camp, beginning with bubblegum-bubble-blowing warmup drills.

different kinds of retail businesses moved in near the arena, while restaurants and sports bars significantly increased their customer numbers, especially on game nights. Local television ratings for the Cavaliers' games went up 300 percent while radio listenership doubled.

James items sold like hotcakes, not only in Cleveland but around the country as well. The gift shop at Gund Arena could barely keep up with the demand for James jerseys and other clothing items. In fact, purchases at the gift shop increased by 500 percent in his rookie year. His number twenty-three jersey by early 2005 was the fifth best-seller among basketball players. In 2004, more than 1.6 million James's jerseys were sold for a total of $72 million.

Cleveland and Akron fans were also thrilled when James announced plans to build himself a huge home in the area. His 5-acre home (2ha), will feature a theater, bowling alley, wall-to-wall television screens, a casino, and a three-story aquarium. While his dream home is being completed, James is splitting his time between a Cleveland apartment and a smaller house in the

Akron area. Cleveland basketball fans take James's home-building plans as an indication that he plans to stay with the Cavaliers. In fact, Cleveland fans are counting on this, as sports writer McCallum wrote, "Already he is an economic system as much as he is an athlete, the primary link in a long chain of dependency. His performance on the court and his comportment off it bear consequences for . . . a city, a franchise, a coach, a general manager, several corporations, and an extended family."[92]

"King James"

After a phenomenal rookie year, James's success in Cleveland continued, and in the three seasons he has since played, he has earned even more honors. "King James," as he is sometimes called, has gathered amazing statistics in all categories and has received even more admiration from professional analysts, players, and coaches. He recently signed a profitable contract extension with the Cavaliers, has been chosen for the 2008 Olympic team, and has become a clever businessman. Still only twenty-three years old, James's future looks limitless.

His Sophomore Season

During his sophomore season (2004–2005), James improved all aspects of his game and led the Cavaliers to their first winning season in years. During that time, he played more minutes per game than anyone else in the league, and also ranked third by scoring a 27.2 average, as well as third in steals, and sixth in assists at 7.2. He became the youngest player in NBA history to record a triple-double (achieving double digit figures in scoring, rebounding, and assisting) and to score fifty points in a single game.

Coach Paul Silas was among the many who praised James's game: "I have never seen a player learn so much in one year. He is further ahead than I thought he would be at this time."[93] During his second season with the Cavaliers, James became one of the NBA's quickest players and best leapers, and earned glowing praise as the undisputed Cavalier team leader.

One of James's greatest assets continued to be his excellent passing. Milwaukee Bucks' forward Desmond Mason commented on this skill: "He really wants to pass and set up his teammates more than anything. Everyone knows he can dunk and score, but he is such a good passer, too. He is hard to guard one-on-one because he is so big and fast. But if you double-team him, he is still just as dangerous with the pass."[94]

In only his second professional season, James was voted to the NBA All-Star team. He thoroughly enjoyed playing with the best players in professional basketball—the other superstars. He played well, scoring thirteen points, handing out eight assists, and capturing six rebounds. James's appearance in this game was only the second appearance for a Cavalier player in the history of their franchise.

By the end of the season, the Cavaliers were fighting for the last playoff spot in the post-season. The team finished with a winning record of 42–40 but failed to qualify for the playoffs.

The Playoffs

During James' third season with the Cavaliers (2005–2006), the team had a 50–32 record and made the play-offs for the first time in eight years. Journalist Sean Deveney reported on the significance: "The first Cavalier playoff game in eight years was not so much about the resurgence of a franchise as it was about James finally playing in the post-season. This was not so much a debut as an unveiling, a revelation, a coronation . . ."[95]

In James' post-season debut against the Washington Wizards, he had thirty-two points, eleven rebounds, and eleven assists. In doing so, he became only the third player in NBA history to have a triple double in a first play-off appearance. He fell just short of another triple-double in the second play-off game, and for the entire series averaged 35.7 points while shooting 50 percent from the field. The Cavaliers defeated the Wizards and advanced to the next play-off round.

After the series was over, Washington Wizard coach Eddie Jordan praised James's skill,

There are two ways to look at it. When you are in single coverage, he breaks you down because he is such a great

In 2006 James helped the Cavaliers make their first play-off in eight years.

player. He can drive to the hoop on you; he can pull up and make a jumper. So you can stay one-on-one on him and guard against the other players. Or you can double him, and, if you do someone is open. He finds people, and then you have no one to handle the rebounding.[96]

Next, the Cavaliers faced the Detroit Pistons, the top-seeded team in the Eastern Conference. After leading the Pistons 3–2 games, however, the Cavaliers failed to win the series, losing the next two games. James's averages, however, were excellent. Their play-off season was over, but the accolades were just beginning. Cavalier General Manager Danny Ferry stated, "The level he's playing at now, I don't know if anyone else is even close."[97]

The World Games

After his appearance in the post-season, James joined a team of American players to participate in the 2006 World Games. Dissatisfied that the United States had not won the gold medal, the Olympic Committee decided to name Duke University basketball coach Mike Krzyzewski as the coach for the 2008 games. Krzyzewski began putting together a stellar team that included James. During practice sessions before the actual games began, Krzyzewski announced that James, Dwayne Wade (Miami Heat), and Carmelo Anthony (Denver Nuggets) would be co-captains of the American team. "It was a pretty easy decision to select those three guys," said the coach.

> From the very start they have asserted themselves and showed leadership through how hard they worked, their cooperation and the fact that they wanted to be like everyone else. They didn't come in as stars, they came in as members of the team. Everyone looks up to them and they look up to them even more now because they have set such a good example.[98]

James commented on his selection, saying "I'm very excited about being a captain because I am a leader. It's a big responsibility

A young fan watches James as he takes a break from the 2006 World Games.

for us three being captains and going out and representing our country in the right way."[99]

In their exhibition games before the championships, the United States team was undefeated in their five appearances, giving them high hopes of winning the actual championship. With the exhibitions over, the team flew to Sapporo, Japan, for an opening game against Puerto Rico. The American team, with James playing a starring role, did well in the first few games, winning by ever-increasing margins. Heading into the semifinal game, the United States looked like a solid bet for the gold medal.

However, despite James's solid performance, the team fell short, losing to Greece in the semifinals, 101–95. A very disappointed American team left the floor with grim faces. Once again, the United States had failed to bring home the gold. Krzyzewski spoke for the team: "We have to learn the international game better. We learned a lot today because we played a team that plays amazing basketball and plays together."[100] The loss also meant that the United States would have to qualify for the 2008 Olympics in the Americas Tournament instead of getting an automatic invitation.

Off the Court

As both an NBA superstar and an Olympian, James has made consistently positive contributions to his teams on the basketball court. He has also made a tremendous impact on the black communities of Cleveland and Akron. According to James, since high school he has wanted to help others who were growing up in similar circumstances to his own. For this reason, he and his family formed the James Family Foundation. According to the foundation's Web site: "The mission of the James Family Foundation is to help children and families (particularly those headed by single parents) achieve more through education, recreation, employment, and better health options."[101]

The James Family Foundation has been successful in raising large sums of money for the underprivileged. They do so, in part, by sponsoring a number of events, including the June 2006 "King for Kids Bike-a-Thon." Proceeds from this event benefited many northeast Ohio programs, including the Akron Urban League and the Akron YMCA. Following the biking, James appeared at an Akron celebration and acknowledged all the people who had come out to support the event. He also donated three hundred brand new Schwinn bicycles to area children. James has always made it a personal priority to appear at all of his charity functions. "What I do with basketball only lasts during the season," James states, "but the work we do with the Foundation goes on nonstop. We want to keep building hopes and dreams in the lives of children and families."[102]

Another annual event that James sponsors is the Back to School Giveaway. With sponsorship by Sam's Club and Target, these events are yet another way in which James is giving back to the community. Chris Dennis, the executive director of the James

Family Foundation, describes the purpose of such events: "The James Family Foundation has recognized that there is a need to provide school supplies to families in northeast Ohio to reduce some of the expenses incurred . . ."[103] During each event, up to one thousand free backpacks filled with school supplies are given away to Akron and Cleveland children. James states, "Education is very important to me, and I will always do what I can to support the kids."[104]

Community Assist Award

In addition to James's philanthropic work in northeast Ohio, he has also been very active elsewhere. James personally donated more than $200,000 worth of relief to Hurricane Katrina victims. He works closely with Boys Hope Girls Hope, an organization that helps place children facing serious family problems and poverty in temporary but more stable living situations. James is particularly interested in this program because of his own experience living with the Walkers. The children involved are facing many of the same challenges that James faced as a child.

To recognize James's efforts in the community, the NBA awarded him with the Community Assist Award in June 2006. The inscription on the plaque that James received, as quoted on NBA.com, stated: "Following the standard set by the NBA Legend David Robinson, who improved the community piece by piece."[1] The NBA, in presenting the award, acknowledged James's donations to the Hurricane Katrina relief efforts, his work with the community, his work with the Make-A-Wish Foundation, and many other philanthropic efforts. The NBA, as a group, participates in many worldwide initiatives, including its work with UNICEF, Habitat for Humanity, and the Boys and Girls Clubs of America.

1 Quoted in Cavaliers. "LeBron James Receives NBA Community Assist Award for June." *NBA.com* July 12, 2006. www.nba.com/cavaliers/community/lbj_community_assist_award_060712.htm

LeBron the Businessman

In addition to his basketball and philanthropic (charitable) work, James has also recently made a number of important business decisions. When James entered the NBA, he hired an agent, Aaron Goodwin, to represent him in all contract negotiations both on and off the court. In 2006, much to the surprise of the basketball world, James fired Goodwin. Shortly thereafter, he announced that he was forming his own management company. While he would be the president of the company, it would be run by his friends Maverick Carter, Randy Mims, and Rich Paul. Mims is James's uncle and the other two are good friends from his high school years.

Microsoft Endorsement

One of the first deals that James's new management company negotiated was a 2007 endorsement with Microsoft Corporation. The software company has launched a new Web site that features a storybook style in which teenagers and youngsters can learn about James's life and career. James has voiced hopes that the Web site will motivate young people around the world to persevere through their own hardships just as he did during his youth.

The Dayton Daily News quotes James, who was excited about the new Web site: "I've always wanted to have a place where kids can see all aspects of my personality—where I can really talk with them about where I came from, what I do, what I have achieved in my life, and what my goals are."[1] James says that another of the Web site's primary purposes will be to help educate young people by offering them challenges and other activities to complete online. James is the first NBA player that Microsoft has used to promote its products.

1 Quoted in "LeBron, Microsoft to Double Team on Interactive Web Site." *Dayton Daily News*, February 20, 2007.

The sports world was shocked, as sports writer Thomaselli comments:

> When Mr. James fired agent Aaron Goodwin, the collective jaws of the NBA and the sports-marketing world dropped. The well-respected Mr. Goodwin had negotiated Mr. James's celebrated 90 million contract with Nike. Then Mr. James did the almost unthinkable in the sometimes stuffy world of sports marketing—he handed his off-the-court business and marketing over to Messrs. Carter, Paul, and Mims.[105]

Sports writers all across the nation thought James was making a huge mistake.

Thus far, the critics have been proved wrong. One of the group's first successes was negotiating a new contract for James with the Cavaliers, reportedly worth $60 million over the next three years. He is now under contract to the Cavaliers through the 2009–2010 season and has an option for a fourth year. James was pleased with the contract extension: "I knew all along—and I had always said—that I wanted to stay here in Cleveland, so it's a terrific day for me and my family to actually make it official."[106]

Despite critics' charges that James was making a huge financial blunder, the decision to start the new company had been solidly thought-out and planned beforehand. The four young men had a vision and a strategic plan that included a new type of sports marketing. Rather than endorsements, James wanted to form partnerships with other companies. They originally called their company Four Horsemen Management, but have since used their first name initials LRMR to refer to their organization. James explained why he made this decision: "I wanted to wake up in the morning and say I did it my way . . . I just wanted to make the decisions."[107] He further commented, "I realized that it was time for me to become a man. I wanted to be like I've always been, the head of everything I've done."[108]

James now talks eagerly of his new marketing company as being a potentially billion-dollar business. James has voiced a desire to top Michael Jordan and become the world's first billion-dollar athlete. The group's ultimate goal is the 2008

Beijing Olympics. By that time, the four men hope to have turned James into a global figure with a number of global endorsements in their pockets. James speaks of this,

> In the next fifteen or twenty years, I hope I'll be the richest man in the world. That's one of my goals. I want to be a billionaire. I want to get to a position where generation on generation don't have to worry about nothing. I don't want family members from my kids to my son's kids to never have to worry. And I can't do that now just playing basketball.[109]

LeBron James—the Father

While James is a superstar on and off the basketball court, perhaps his greatest satisfaction today comes from being a father. On October 6, 2004, James and his longtime girlfriend, Savannah Brinson, had a child together—LeBron James Jr. He and Brinson are raising the child together. As a father, he appreciates even more the sacrifices his mother made to raise him. He states: "Now that I have a son, I have no idea how she did it by herself because I couldn't do it by myself. She taught me through all the trials and tribulations. She's by far my greatest influence. She gets all the credit. I don't know how, but she did it."[110]

LeBron credits his son with helping him mature and making him more aware of the kind of man he wants to be. He wants to be a good father and a solid presence in his son's life. During warm-ups before Cavalier games, James can often be spotted cradling his child and kissing him. He talks about how being a father has enlightened him:

> It's great. Sometimes in the past when I played, something might make me lose focus, or I would go home after a game where I thought I could have played better, and I would let it hang over my head for a long time when it shouldn't. But now, being a parent, I go home and see my son and I forget

James is not reluctant to show affection to his son, LeBron Jr., in breaks from Cavalier warm-ups.

LeBron and longtime girlfriend Savannah Brinson have had two children together.

about any mistake I ever made or the reason I'm upset. I get home and my son is smiling or he comes running to me. It has just made me grow as an individual and grow as a man.[111]

During the 2007 post-season, James and Brinson welcomed a second son, Bryce Maximus James, who was born on June 14, 2007.

His Legacy

With solid performances on and off the court, James's future looks bright. Even though James is only twenty-three years old, analysts and reporters have already begun to talk about his basketball legacy. Many believe him to be one of the best three or four players in the NBA today. Coach Jeff Van Gundy of the Houston Rockets summed up James' potential: ". . . He's got poise. He's got presence. He's got vision. He's got command of his game. He's one of those guys who's just an intelligent basketball player. On top of being a superior talent. So, what do you have? You've got greatness."[112] Sports analysts point out that during each of his NBA seasons, James has continued to improve his game. "He's climbed to the top of the mountain very quickly," writes sports writer Michael Lee. "With the hype he got coming in, it was hard to imagine that he could've lived up to it. He's surpassed it."[113] James is, according to most players, coaches, and analysts, the best small forward in the league. He is also favorably compared to some of the greatest stars who have ever played. According to former NBA coach Hubie Brown, James ". . . never ceases to amaze me. The things that he does offensively just blow you away."[114]

And yet, despite James's success on the basketball court, many sports analysts are unwilling to place him among the best players in NBA history. Most believe that he will ultimately be judged on how many championships he wins for the Cavaliers. Many feel that he needs to do what Michael Jordan did—dominate basketball and eventually win a championship. Sports writer

James makes a spectacular dunk.

Marty Burns writes, "LeBron James has the talent. He has the TV commercials. He even has the nickname 'King James.' But he doesn't yet own any championship bling."[115] Another basketball player, Eric Snow, weighed in with his opinion: "You can't take away anything he's accomplished. But in order for him to go down as a great player, he needs to show leadership on a championship team. This is where he proves himself."[116]

LeBron James's Achievements and Firsts

During his four-year professional basketball career, LeBron James has already amassed an amazing number of "firsts." His achievements on the court are all the more noteworthy because of his young age. His accomplishments include:

- Youngest player to be named Rookie of the Year at age nineteen.
- Youngest player to record a triple double.
- Youngest player to score fifty points in one game—he did this on March 20, 2005, when he scored fifty-six points in a losing effort against the Toronto Raptors.
- Youngest player to score 2,000 points in one season (2004–05); to average 30 points in a season (2005–06); as well as the youngest to reach 1,000, 2,000, 3,000, 4,000, 5,000, 6,000, and 7,000 points.
- Youngest player to win an All-Star game Most Valuable Player award and the youngest to be named to the all-NBA first team. He was the youngest player to ever lead the entire league in All-Star voting (2007) and the youngest to be named to an American Olympic team.

He has also won countless awards: 2004 Rookie of the Year; 2004 ESPY Best Breakthrough Athlete, 2006 All-Star MVP, two-time NBA All Star. He was also named the 2005–2006 *The Sporting News* co-MVP with Steve Nash.

Success has made James one of the superstars of the basketball world. Yet it is often difficult for any person to live up to others' expectations of them. Few other individuals have had as many expectations placed on them as James did, but James has met those expectations and, in many cases, exceeded them. He has done so with natural talent and humility. James remains humble, "To this day, I don't feel it," he says, when asked about when he knew he was a superstar. "I hear my friends and my mom tell me I'm special, but honestly, I still don't get it. I just want to be levelheaded about things. I think about the times I had before and I don't want to go back to those times."[117]

Introduction: A Prodigy

1. Michelle Kaufman. "At 17, LeBron James Ponders His NBA Future."*Knight Ridder/Tribune News Service*, December 2, 2002.
2. Ryan Jones. *King James: Believe the Hype: The LeBron James Story*. New York: St. Martin's Press, 2003, p. 16.
3. Quoted in David Lee Morgan. *LeBron James: The Rise of a Star*. Cleveland: Gray and Company, 2003, p. 9.

Chapter 1: Overcoming Poverty and Deprivation

4. Jock Bio. "LeBron James." Jock Bio. www.jockbio.com/Bios/James/James_bio.html.
5. Quoted in Jack McCallum. "You Gotta Carry That Weight." *Sports Illustrated*, October 27, 2003, p. 74.
6. Morgan. *LeBron James*, p. 17.
7. Quoted in Morgan. *LeBron James*, p. 20.
8. Jones. *King James*, p. 22.
9. Morgan. *LeBron James*, p. 25.
10. Quoted in Tom Withers. "Formative Years Mold LeBron James the Man." *AP Online*, December 10, 2005.
11. Jock Bio. "LeBron James."
12. Jones. *King James*, p. 23.
13. Quoted in Morgan. *LeBron James*, p. 33.
14. Quoted in Morgan. *LeBron James*, p. 86.
15. Quoted in Morgan. *LeBron James*, p. 39.
16. "Amateur Athletic Union." *AAU*. http://aausports.org
17. Quoted in "About LeBron James." *LeBron James*. www.acting/modeling.com/celebs/lebron_james.htm
18. Quoted in Morgan. *LeBron James*, p. 46.

Chapter 2: The Chosen One

19. Quoted in Jones. *King James*, p. 31.
20. Quoted in Morgan. *LeBron James*, p. 54
21. Quoted in Morgan. *LeBron James*, p. 85.

22. Quoted in Jones. *King James*, p. 34.
23. Quoted in Jones. *King James*, p. 91.
24. Quoted in Morgan. *LeBron James*, p. 60.
25. Quoted in Terry Pluto. "LeBron James, Once a Lanky Kid, Has Come a Long Way in the NBA." *Akron Beacon Journal*, April 20, 2004.
26. Quoted in Morgan. *LeBron James*, p. 74.
27. Quoted in Jones. *King James*, p. 81.
28. Quoted in Jones. *King James*, p. 60.
29. Jones. *King James*, p. 42.
30. Quoted in Jones. *King James*, p. 87.
31. Quoted in Jones. *King James*, p. 100.
32. Scott Fowler. "Still in High School, James has EBay, NBA Circling." *Knight Ridder/Tribune News Service*, December 10, 2002.
33. Quoted in Morgan. *LeBron James*, p. 92.
34. Jones. *King James*, p. 125.
35. Jones. *King James*, p. 106.
36. Quoted in Morgan. *LeBron James*, p. 87.
37. Quoted in Jones. *King James*, p. 140.

Chapter 3: Believe the Hype

38. Quoted in Gordon. *Tales from the Cleveland Cavaliers*, p. 26.
39. Jones. *King James*, p. 139.
40. Kaufman. "At 17, LeBron James Ponders His NBA Future."
41. Quoted in Michael Rand. "Sold! The Selling of Prep Basketball Star LeBron James." *Minneapolis Star Tribune*, January 26, 2003.
42. Rand. "Sold!"
43. Quoted in Kaufman. "At 17, LeBron James Ponders His NBA Future."
44. Quoted in Fowler. "Still in High School."
45. Quoted in Kaufman. "At 17, LeBron James Ponders His NBA Future."
46. Quoted in Kevin Horrigan. "Deposed LeBron James a Commodity at Very Young Age." *Knight Ridder/Tribune News Service*, January 31, 2003.
47. Quoted in Morgan. *LeBron James*, p. 96.

48. Quoted in Morgan. *LeBron James*, p. 107.

49. Rand. "Sold! The Selling of Prep Basketball Star LeBron James."

50. Jones. *King James*, p. 21.

51. Quoted in Morgan. *LeBron James*, p.12.

52. Marty Burns. "Believe the Hype." *SI.com* December 12, 2002. http://sportsillustrated.cnn.com/inside_game/marty_burns/news/2002/12/12/burns_james_sp

53. Quoted in Tom Withers. "LeBron James Cleared in Hummer Inquiry." *AP Online*, January 28, 2003.

54. Quoted in Morgan. *LeBron James*, p. 125.

55. Quoted in David Lee Morgan Jr. "LeBron James Returns Jersey to Store." *Knight Ridder/Tribune News Service*, February 1, 2003.

56. Quoted in Morgan. "LeBron James Returns Jersey to Store."

57. Quoted in Morgan. *LeBron James*, p. 139.

58. Quoted in Jones. *King James*, p. 11.

59. Quoted in Morgan. *LeBron James*, p. 64.

60. Quoted in Morgan. *LeBron James*, p. 106.

61. Jockbio. "LeBron James."

62. Quoted in Kaufman. "At 17, LeBron James Ponders His NBA Future."

63. Jones. *King James*, p. 184.

64. Quoted in Jones. *King James*, p. 184.

Chapter 4: Rookie Sensation

65. Kaufman. "At 17, LeBron James Ponders His NBA Future."

66. Morgan. *LeBron James*, p. 152.

67. Tom Withers. "Nike Gives LeBron James $90 Million Deal." *AP Online*, May 23, 2003.

68. Quoted in Withers. "Nike Gives LeBron James $90 Million Deal."

69. Quoted in Gordon. *Tales from the Cleveland Cavaliers*, p. 22.

70. Quoted in Gordon. *Tales from the Cleveland Cavaliers*, p. 9.

71. Quoted in Gordon. *Tales from the Cleveland Cavaliers*, p. 133.

72. Quoted in Mark Murphy. "The Phenom: Say Hello to the NBA's Teenage Idol, Cleveland's LeBron James." *Boston Herald*, November 14, 2003.

73. Quoted in McCallum. "You Gotta Carry that Weight," p. 73.

74. Quoted in Murphy. "The Phenom."

75. McCallum. "You Gotta Carry that Weight," p. 70.

76. Jockbio. "LeBron James."

77. Quoted in McCallum. "You Gotta Carry that Weight," p. 70.

78. Quoted in Dwain Price. "It's Good to be the King." *Fort Worth Star-Telegram*, February 20, 2005.

79. Gordon. *Tales from the Cleveland Cavaliers*, p. 28.

80. Arana Lynch. "The Impact of LeBron James's Star-Power on the Black Community." *Cleveland Call and Post*, November 19, 2003.

81. Quoted in Murphy. "The Phenom."

82. Quoted in Pluto. "LeBron James, Once a Lanky Kid."

83. Gordon. *Tales from the Cleveland Cavaliers*, p. 101.

84. Jockbio. "LeBron James."

85. Quoted in Gordon. *Tales from the Cleveland Cavaliers*, p. 116.

86. Jockbio. "LeBron James."

87. Quoted in Gordon. *Tales from the Cleveland Cavaliers*, p. 116.

88. Quoted in Murphy. "The Phenom."

89. Sports Illustrated. "LeBron Adds Athens to Offseason Travel Plans." *Si.com*, May 14, 2004. http://sportsillustrated.cnn.com/2004/basketball/nba/05/14/olympics

90. Jockbio. "LeBron James."

91. Gordon. *Tales from the Cleveland Cavaliers*, p. 134.

92. McCallum. "You Gotta Carry that Weight," p. 70.

Chapter 5: "King James"

93. Quoted in Sean Deveney."Crystal Baller: LeBron James's Uncanny Ability to See What's Coming is Keeping Him a Step Ahead of the Competition." *The Sporting News*, December 20, 2004.

94. Quoted in Deveney. "Crystal Baller."

95. Sean Deveney. "The Man Who Would Be King." *The Sporting News*, May 5, 2006.

96. Deveney. "The Man Who Would Be King."

97. Quoted in Michael Lee. "How Will LeBron Make His Mark?" *The Washington Post*, April 16, 2006.

98. Quoted in ESPN. "LeBron, 'Melo, Wade Named Team USA Captains." *ESPN.com*, August 17, 2006. http://sports.espn. go.com/oly/wbc2006/news/story?id=2552772

99. Quoted in ESPN. "LeBron, 'Melo, Wade Named Team USA Captains."

100. Quoted in ESPN. "Upset Special: Greece Stuns US in FIBA Semis." *ESPN.com*, September 1, 2006. http://sports.espn. go.com/oly/wbc2006/news/story?id=2568543

101. Quoted in Cavaliers. "James Family Foundation to Host Back to School Giveaways with Sam's Club." *NBA.com*, August 8, 2006. www.nba.com/cavaliers.news/lbj_school_ shop_060818.html

102. Quoted in Cavaliers. "LeBron James Receives NBA Community Assist Award for Junes." *NBA.com*, July 12, 2006. www.nba.com/cavaliers/community/lbj_community_ assist_award_060712.html

103. Quoted in Cavaliers. "James Family Foundation to Host Back to School Giveaways with Target." *NBA.com* August 29, 2006. www.nba.com/cavaliers/community/james_ backtoschool_050829.html

104. Quoted in Cavaliers. "James Family Foundation to Host Back to School Giveaways with Sam's Club."

105. Rich Thomaselli. "All the King's Men." *Advertising Age*, July 17, 2006.

106. Quoted in Associated Press. "LeBron Gets $60 Million from Cavs." *Associated Press*, July 12, 2006.

107. Quoted in Thomaselli. "All the King's Men."

108. Quoted in Withers. "Formative Years Mold LeBron James the Man."

109. Quoted in Withers. "Formative Years Mold LeBron James the Man."

110. Quoted in . "Formative Years Mold LeBron James the Man."

111. Quoted in Withers. "Formative Years Mold LeBron James the Man."

112. Quoted in Gordon. *Tales from the Cleveland Cavaliers.* P. 39.

113. Quoted in Lee. "How Will LeBron Make His Mark?"

114. Quoted in Deveney. "The Man Who Would Be King."

115. Burns. "Believe the Hype."

116. Quoted in Deveney. "The Man Who Would Be King."

117. Quoted in Withers. "Formative Years Mold LeBron James the Man."

December 30, 1984

LeBron Raymone James is born in Akron, Ohio.

Fall 1994

LeBron plays organized basketball for the first time. He is nine years old.

Spring 2001, 2002, 2003

LeBron named Mr. Basketball of Ohio for the first time in 2001. The award is given to the best high school player in Ohio. He is named again in 2002 and 2003, making him the only high school basketball player to win this honor three times.

February 18, 2002

LeBron appears on the cover of *Sports Illustrated*.

January 2003

LeBron is involved in two potential scandals—the Hummer incident and the jersey incident.

May 2003

James signs a multimillion dollar deal with Nike.

June 6, 2003

James is the first player chosen in the National Basketball Association draft.

June 2004

James is named Rookie of the Year in the NBA.

Summer 2004

James is named to the U.S. Men's Basketball Olympic Team but sees limited action.

2005–2006 season

James leads the Cavaliers to his first play-off experience.

Summer 2006

James is named captain of the U.S. men's basketball team for the World Games and leads the team to a third-place finish.

2006–2007 season

LeBron leads the Cavaliers to another play-off season.

For More Information

Books

Jeff Savage. *LeBron James*. Minneapolis: Lerner Publications, 2006. This book for younger readers offers a brief biography of the superstar.

Web Sites

Associated Press. "Cavaliers' James Will Appear in Microsoft Ad Campaign." *MSNBC.com* January 24, 2007. www.msnbc.msn.com/id/16780008

Marty Burns. "Dynasty Builder?" *SI.com* November 1, 2006. http://sportsillustrated.cnn.com/2006/writers/marty_burns/10/31/lebron.dynasty

ESPN. "LeBron Leads US in Final Tuneup Rout of Korea." *ESPN.com* August 15, 2006. http://sports.espn.go.com/oly/wbc2006/news/story?id=2549894

ESPN. "US Runs Past China, Improves to 2-0 at Worlds." *ESPN.com* August 21, 2006. http://sports.espn.go.com/oly/wbc2006/news/story?id=2555289

"LeBron James." *LeBron James: Cleveland Cavaliers.* http://lebronjamesleb.tripod.com

LeBron James. *Cleveland Plain Dealer.* www.cleveland.com/cavs This website from the *Cleveland Plain Dealer* newspaper presents the latest news about James.

"LeBron James." *LeBron James: Information from Answers.com.* www.answers.com/topic.lebron-james

LeBron James. *Microsoft.* www.lebron.msn.com This website offers a storybook style site about James's life and career.

"LeBron James Biography." *LeBron James: The Unofficial Fan Site.* www.lebron-james.us/biography.html

"School Days." *School Days LeBron James.* http://lebron.wetpaint.com/page/School%20Days

Periodicals

"Prep Superstar LeBron James Ruled Ineligible Because of Jersey Issue." *Akron Beacon Journal*, January 31, 2003.

PR Newswire. "Nike Announces LeBron James Asia Tour Summer 2005. *PR Newswire*, July 8, 2005.

Tom Withers. "Nike Gives LeBron James $90M Deal." *AP Online*. May 23, 2003.

National Public Radio

Bob Edwards. "Profile: Popularity Surrounding High School Basketball Star LeBron James." *NPR*, December 25, 2002.

Cover: © Ron Schwane/Reuters/Corbis

AP Images, 9, 13, 16, 18, 28, 35, 42, 46, 49, 50, 51, 57, 60, 63, 65, 68, 75, 77, 83, 86

© Cadbury Adams/Handout /X00272/Reuters/Corbis, 71

© Fred Prouser/Reuters/Corbis, 84

© Hunter Martin/Corbis, 58

© Michael J. Lebrecht, II/Time Inc., 36

© Royalty-free/Shutterstock, Inc., 12

Anne Wallace Sharp is the author of the adult book *Gifts*, a compilation of stories about hospice patients; several children's books, including *Daring Pirate Women*; and eleven other Thomson-Gale books. In addition, she has written numerous magazine articles for both the adult and juvenile markets. A retired registered nurse, Sharp has a degree in history. Her other interests include reading, traveling, and spending time with her grandchildren, Jacob and Nicole. Sharp lives in Beavercreek, Ohio.